917.43 818
Wolf, Marguerite
I'll take the back road.

W9-BVB-605

DISCARD

I'll Take the Back Road

I'll Take the Back Road

MARGUERITE HURREY WOLF

Drawings by Robert MacLean

The
Stephen
Greene
Press
Brattleboro,
Vermont

The author is happy to acknowledge the cooperation of Holt, Rinehart and Winston and Jonathan Cape Limited, publishers, and the Estate of Robert Frost, the editor, in allowing her to quote lines from "The Tuft of Flowers" from *The Poetry of Robert Frost* edited by Edward Connery Lathem. Copyright 1934, © 1969 by Holt, Rinehart and Winston, Inc. Copyright © 1962 by Robert Frost. Reprinted by permission of Holt, Rinehart and Winston, publishers; of Walter Hard for permission to reprint the lines of poetry on page 10 from "Arrival" in *A Matter of Fifty Houses,* by Walter Hard, copyright 1952 by Walter Hard, The Vermont Book Shop, Middlebury, Vermont; and of the Vermont Development Commission for permission to reprint "Grounded by a Grouse," which was previously published in the Spring, 1975, issue of *Vermont Life* magazine. Copyright © 1975 by Vermont Life Magazine.

Portions of this book were originally published as *Anything Can Happen in Vermont.*

This book has been produced in the United States of America: designed by R. L. Dothard Associates, composed by American Book–Stratford Press, and printed and bound by The Colonial Press. It is published by The Stephen Greene Press, Brattleboro, Vermont 05301.

Library of Congress Cataloging in Publication Data

Wolf, Marguerite Hurrey.
   I'll take the back road.
   Portions published in 1965 under title: Anything can happen in Vermont.
   Essays.
   1. Vermont—Social life and customs. 2. Vermont—Description and travel—1951–   3. Country life—Vermont. 4. Wolf, Marguerite Hurrey. I. Title.
F55.W6   1975   974.3   74–27458
ISBN 0–8289–0244–5 917.43

75 76 77 78 79 80 81 9 8 7 6 5 4 3 2 1

For the two new members of our family,
Adrienne Philips and Tage Strom

Contents

Prologue

SHORTLY after we moved away from Vermont eleven years ago I wrote an article called "Good-bye and Keep Cold," which began: "I suppose that time will cure our homesickness for Vermont."

Well, it didn't. Of course we never left Vermont completely. We still owned the small hillside farm in Jericho which we bought in 1948 and we have returned each summer whether our winter address was Boston or Kansas City. Time didn't cure our homesickness but we didn't realize until we returned to stay that time does dim the colors and dull the sharpness of remembered images.

And now we are back, not just for a vacation but to live here in all five seasons, to plant a garden each Memorial Day, build a new house and make our whole life here or perhaps I mean make our life whole by living here.

What did we miss and what did we hope to find again in Vermont when we returned? Space and time. Space in which to be alone together and time to see old friends and pursue new interests. Fewer people in large groups and more people as individuals. Communication instead of confrontation. Mowing, or not, our own lawn, cleaning our own house, growing and preserving a part of our own food and, most of all, living in close combat and harmony with the changing seasons. We came back on May 7 and it snowed. But the grass that poked through the snow was the most brilliant green I have ever seen, because of the contrast. Asparagus spears were just showing amethyst tips through the moist earth that steamed in the sun. I had forgotten how lacy the

Prologue

shad blossoms were and that our old semi-reclining apple trees leafed so far out before they blossomed, a mist of green as background for the tight pink buds. I had forgotten that dandelions by the meadowful can be enjoyed with no compulsion to stalk them individually. The gradual unfolding of spring allows time to see, with Robert Frost, that "nature's first green is gold" flowing along the willow wands and lighting the sugar maples while the muted reds of the swamp maples and osiers repeat the vibrant scarlet and crimson of October.

We rediscovered the various greens and the fragrance of Vermont summer; drying hay, honey locust, red clover and milkweed, heavy-sweet. But who besides the bees celebrates the fragrance of milkweed? Other odors, pungent but part of the essence of summer, freshly manured fields, marigolds and that strange green smell of tomato plants which rubs off on your hands when you touch the vines. Dill, cucumber and vinegar together. And the sounds of summer, the clacking of a combine, the papery conversation in the corn patch, the crack of a bat against a ball and the adolescent twittering of barn swallows on the telephone wires too early in the morning.

Everyone knows that fall in Vermont is almost too chromatic to believe and some of the wider highways are lined with cars full of people who are out to have their credulity tested. But there are still miles of country roads winding through evergreen forests and incandescent tree tunnels of maples, occasionally passing a farm, a white church, a Post Office and General Store combined. There are sudden views from hilltop clearings out across valleys that still support more cows than people and sometimes neither one. After four years in the midwest we marvel at the variety in the Vermont landscape, which we merely accepted when we lived here. Losing something for a while enhances its value when it is found, whether it is the sound of rain on the roof after a long drought, the taste of a sun-ripened tomato after our long winter of discontent with the plastic substitutes in the supermarkets, or the satisfaction from planting and defending a vegetable garden.

"But what about the winters?" our friends asked. "You are older now and haven't skied in years. You've been living in a much milder climate for a long time."

Yes, we haven't shoveled or skidded or even shivered very much in the past nine years but neither have we enjoyed the frost patterns on the window panes, the purple shadows on the mountains, expanses of untrammeled snow or the comfort of sitting in front of an open fire while the wind spits snow against the windows. It comes back again to contrasts. You have to be cold to appreciate warmth. And to step from a warm house into a clear cold night is exhilarating with the bite and sweetness of an apple just picked from the tree. When I think of unpleasant winter weather I think of cities. I have been colder in Boston, New York and Chicago, especially Chicago, than I have ever been in Vermont, no matter what the thermometer said.

If winter seems reluctant to leave in March or April I will remember that its persistence enhances our excitement over the first concert by the peepers. The sight of snow fences being rolled up or the curl of fragrant steam rising from the sugarhouses lifts the winter-weary spirit.

Now, more than ten years after our departure, we have come back to Vermont. We're glad we did. Vermont has changed some but so have we and not always for the better in either case. But the unique things about Vermont are scarcer all over the world these days and finding them here again makes it seem even better than we remembered. When

Prologue

so many fundamental values are being questioned, debated and ditched, only nature is enduring, and independence, for which Vermonters have always been famous, can come only from the responsibility of working in harness with her. We like it that way and that is why we have come back—for *good!*

Jericho Center, Vermont, 1974   M. H. W.

Vermont & Vermonters

On Becoming a Vermonter

WE did not come to Vermont because of ancestral ties. At that time we were unaware that we could claim any north of the George Washington Bridge. Nor did we come because of a love of skiing. We lost what little we had of that the first winter. My husband was a physician in New York City. We lived in an apartment in mid-Manhattan where the car appeared automatically when summoned on the house phone, and the elevator operators considered dogs to be more chic than children.

We came to Vermont because of a yearning to balance our dependent and mechanized winter life with the more self-reliant and simpler pattern of country ways. So we bought a little farm in the northern part of the state, seventeen acres, more or less (more rocks and less soil), a Christmas card brook and waterfall, and a very old house which only its owners could love. For five summers we worked off our need to return to the soil by planting a large vegetable garden, keeping twelve hens, two pigs and a pair of kittens, and painting more board feet of old porous wood than I care to remember.

This provided the children with cheap vacations and an enviable source of material of "experience-sharing" discussions at school. It gave their parents aching backs, calloused hands, and a string of funny anecdotes with which to bore their friends all winter.

Just as we were beginning to realize that our lives were more split than our personalities, a kindly fate nudged the University of Vermont into asking my husband to be dean of the Medical College, and we moved to Vermont forever, as it seemed at that time.

"Now," I thought, "we shall be real Vermonters." No more wincing at the tinge of condescension in the term "summer folks." The hens would not have to be dressed off by Labor Day. The pigs could grow to maturity before butchering, and the children would climb aboard a yellow school bus.

It was rather fun being a new Vermonter for a while. I was forgiven for planting asparagus roots upside down and returning a pie plate empty. But, as year after year went by, it troubled me that we were still considered novices. We had been humored, watched, and finally accepted on the sole basis of our desire and increasing ability to do our own chores and repairs. But we were not Vermonters.

One July afternoon, shelling peas on the lawn, while our oldest Vermont friend sat nearby scratching the necks of our latest and most beautiful kittens, I shyly asked him if our children would ever be real Vermonters.

"No," he said, burying his face in the kittens' soft fur. "Can't say they will."

"But why not?" I asked. "They were so young when they came here. They speak like the other children, look like them, go to the same school, wear the same clothes."

"Well," he mused, looking off to the hills as though in search of some kind way to explain this obvious truth to one forever beyond the pale, "it's this way. If the mother cat jumped into your oven and had these kittens in the stove, you wouldn't call them biscuits, would you?"

How Did You Happen
to Come to Vermont?

IF there is one favorite question for the born Vermonter to put to the adopted Vermonter, it is, "How did you happen to come to Vermont?"

Like the child who begs, "Tell me about when I was a baby," the one asking the question hopes for an answer which will make him feel loved and important. Because in Vermont the personality of the state is also the personality of the people.

I enjoy being asked this question, no matter how often, because I know that through my answer both the born Vermonter (who cared enough to ask) and the adopted Vermonter (who cared enough to come) will be warmed by mutual approval of themselves and of the Vermont tradition. Most Vermonters don't talk about the Vermont tradition; they live it. Dorothy Canfield Fisher did both, with exquisite understatement. "Vermont tradition is based on the idea that group life should leave each person as free as possible to arrange his own life. This freedom is the only climate in which (we feel) a human being may create his own happiness. . . . Character itself lies deep and secret below the surface, unknown and unknowable by others. It is the mysterious core of life, which every man or woman has to cope with alone, to live with, to conquer and put in order, or to be defeated by."

Our nearest neighbor is a dairy farmer, a good one. His cows are well cared-for and his barn is clean. But, on a crisp

5

Vermont & Vermonters

October day, he and his wife get into the car—or the truck, if their son has taken the car to school—and go off with a picnic lunch to see the foliage. Or in the spring they'll follow the turbulent brooks in hip boots, trout fishing, or maybe drive all the way to Hardwick to see the tulips. His wife is Catholic. He is Protestant. And neither one has ever asked me about my faith. In fact, in all the years since we became year-round Vermonters, we have never been urged to join any church, though my husband knows several of the ministers, the rabbi, and the Catholic bishop as well as he knows some of his medical colleagues.

The truth is no one just happens to come to Vermont except the born Vermonter. Most of the rest of us have been drawn by a magnetic force which added impetus to some economic reason for coming. A family moves where the husband's job is. But these moves are seldom without an element of choice. Since we have lived in Vermont my husband has had a good many offers of interesting, well-paying jobs in different parts of the country, and only once or twice has he been intrigued enough to weigh the pros and cons.

And do you know what has been the deciding factor holding him here? Vermont, the opportunities Vermont gives him to do a certain kind of job, both local and national; the way we are able to live and the alternately stimulating and tranquilizing effect of living close to the cycle of the seasons.

More than thirty years ago my husband and I, on a quick trip through Vermont, stopped on the crest of French Hill at sunset. We looked out over the Winooski Valley suffused with pale chartreuse light and he announced, "Someday I will live in this valley."

Ten years later, one rainy day, while we lived in Manhattan, I gave a ride to an acquaintance who was on her way to place an ad in the *Saturday Review* offering her converted

How Did You Happen to Come to Vermont?

barn in Underhill, Vermont, for rent. The ad was never printed. We rented the barn and spent a month hunting for a summer home in that area. Two days before we had to return to New York, we drove through Jericho Center and stopped at the combined General Store and Post Office. Mr. Nealy happened to ask what brought us there, and maybe it just happened that his father's abandoned farm with the most beautiful natural pool in the world was exactly what we had been looking for. More than a year later we discovered that our little farm was in the valley we had seen from French Hill.

Maybe it just happened that some former colleagues of my husband at Cornell were on the faculty of the Medical College. Because we were in Vermont and they happened to be on the committee to find a new dean, something prompted them to suggest my husband's name as a candidate.

We certainly didn't plan it that way. We had just bought a house in Westchester. I came up to Burlington with my husband for the interviews only so that I could go out to the farm in Jericho and cut down our Christmas tree to take back to the city.

There was no way to warn me that the committee had decided to meet the candidate's wife. Perhaps they wanted to be sure that these city folk were adaptable to the Vermont climate. So it just happened that being an indifferent woodsman in gnawing down the Yule tree, I had covered myself with pitch, snow and dirt. Bundled in scarf, boots and an old hunting cap, flushed with victory and exertion, I clumped into the lobby of the Hotel Vermont and was brought up short by a barricade of the outstretched hands of the committee. They were stuck with me, quite literally.

It didn't just happen that we bought the hundred-and-fifty-year-old farmhouse three miles south and east of Burlington instead of the ranch-type or Victorian dungeon-type we had been looking at in town. We just liked it better. And we had a good reason for insulating the attic. The oil bill was too high. The old letters and papers found between the attic joists had not been put there one hundred years before to wait for us. They were probably put there for the same reason that made George stuff insulation between the boards. But a few months later Mr. Lynn Tracy just happened to take a sentimental journey from Chicago to our house, where his ancestors had lived. Why, of all the Fay descendants, was he the only one who knew all about the family and had collected other letters and urged me to bring to life the ghosts who had remained in the attic until we carried them downstairs in a bushel basket?

I am no fatalist. Maybe these things happen more easily in Vermont. And the reason for this goes back to Mrs. Fisher's statement that Vermont tradition is based on the idea that group life should leave each person as free as possible to arrange his own life.

In the Vermont climate (emotional climate, I mean, though the physical climate humbles or inspires us daily) we find freedom to choose our way of life, to work in the city and live in the country, to raise our own pigs and chickens but cook them in an electric oven, to drive to a tea in the pickup truck or enlist the aid of a visiting dignitary in setting up the chicken brooder, without ever encountering a raised eyebrow. I am "helped" in stores as politely when I am clad in sneakers as when I am shod in Capezios, which did not happen on upper Fifth Avenue. Why, I even planted those asparagus roots upside down under the nose of an experienced gardener without criticism because he figured they were our asparagus roots!

We have had space to stand off from ourselves a bit and

8

decide what things are important. And we have rediscovered the assurance that comes, sometimes when you are picking apples or walking through the snowy woods, from realizing the most important thing is that natural forces are stronger and more enduring than man's bungling attempts to alter them. The bluets will follow the patches of snow under these pines in spite of world crises created by men. Our apple tree will hang heavy with fruit, and then with ice, and then again with a foam of blossom.

Ninety-two acres, as it was in South Burlington or seventeen acres, as it is in Jericho, more or less, and eternity to boot.

You Take the Highway:
I'll Take the Back Way

IF you prefer a smooth wide road where you can cruise steadily at the legal limit in all seasons, stay on the interstate highway. In fact I wish all the tourists would so that we rural types could enjoy our golden tree tunnels and silent arches of snow-laden pines in quiet. But from the advent of the first Model T, the questing tourist has managed to get himself lost on Vermont back roads and has unwittingly provided Vermonters with anecdotes to evoke chuckles from their neighbors at the General Store or Post Office.

Walter Hard captured one of these moments in his poem when octogenarian Steve Henderson, ruminating quietly on the Post Office steps, was accosted by a baffled traveler.

> *"Can you tell me how to get to Stockbridge Corners?"*
> *"Nope."*
> *"You mean you can't tell me how to get to Stockbridge*
> *   Corners?"*
> *"Nope."*
> *"Would you mind telling me why you can't give me this*
> *   information?"*
> *Steve humped his shoulders and twisted his face*
> *Into his nearest approach to a smile*
> *Firing (tobacco juice) again and then chewing rapidly*
> *   he said,*
> *"B'gol you're there."*

10

You Take the Highway: I'll Take the Back Way

It might have been the same store where a touring car full of summer folk stopped to inquire the way to the Blodgett farm. The storekeeper of course knew where the Blodgetts lived and exactly how to get there.

"Go ten miles until you come to a covered bridge. Take the turn three miles before you reach the bridge. When you go up their road if you come to a white church, you've gone too far."

In the early days when the little Morgan mares could maneuver through mud that mired the carriages and wagons, the census around the cracker barrel was usually reduced to those within walking distance of the store. News traveled slowly and the farther the raconteur had to walk, the more time he had to embellish his story.

Eben Fuller clumped up the steps of the store and all heads around the stove turned towards the door, hoping for a bit of verbal refreshment.

"Morning, Eben, what's new up your way?"

"Not too much. I just passed Foster Davis' hat down in the mud waller."

"Where was Foster?"

"Well, his head and shoulders were right there, under the hat, but he was up to his waist in mud."

"Reckon we should get a team and haul him out?"

"No, by Judast, I don't. I ast him did he want a hist and he said, 'What fer? I still got my horse under me.'"

The expression "You can't get there from here" is funny only to those "from away." The back roads usually followed the path of least resistance. Inasmuch as the resistance is the state-long Green Mountain range, there are a good many locations where you can't get from a town on the western side of Vermont to the parallel one in the Connecticut valley without detouring a hundred miles to the nearest gap. Most

13

of the roads run north and south avoiding the mountains or following a stream. But occasionally a road will make a loop that lengthens its route for no apparent reason. One example was right in front of our house in South Burlington. It would have been more direct for Hinesburg Road to slant northwest from the Wright Farm past our house toward Burlington. Instead, it went close to Rollin Tilley's house and then turned sharply west. The explanation turned up in an old record. Rollin's house had been a tavern shortly after the Revolution when the road was being hacked out by every able-bodied man along its route. The tavern keeper saw that the proposed (more direct) route would divert travelers from his hostelry so he offered the work crew a keg of rum and a keg of Holland gin to dog-leg the new road right through his dooryard.

Ralph Hill tells my favorite back road story with suitable straight-faced understatement.

A tourist stopped at a fork in the road where both signs read "To Londonderry." Mystified by this ambivalence he noticed a farmer plowing in the adjoining field and waiting until he was within earshot he shouted, "Does it matter which road I take to Londonderry?"

The farmer finished his row, studied the tourist at length, turned the plow and starting back down the next furrow, called out over his shoulder, "Not to me, it doesn't!"

The Vermont Image

WE have such a stereotyped image of regional types that the summer visitor to Vermont feels cheated out of his birthright to Yankee tradition and local color if those who live between the Connecticut River and Lake Champlain cannot be recognized as Vermonters at twenty paces. For nearly two hundred years the average American has insisted that the Vermonter is a lean, taciturn septuagenarian, crackling with dry wit and with a face that was chiseled from the granite quarries in Barre. He not only must be a dyed-in-the-wool Republican, a more or less active member of the Congregational Church, but also directly descended from that gregarious group who squeezed onto the decks of the *Mayflower* or at least the *Speedwell*.

The Vermonter is not a myth. He can be found in most I.G.A. stores or steaming through the long day of Town Meeting in the Grange Hall or baiting his fellow legislators on the porch of the renovated Pavilion in Montpelier. He has not retired to the hills to wage war on mankind, but he has often moved into town and sold his farm to another Vermonter who is the more common variety, at least in the northern part of the state if not in the popular image.

Such a Vermonter is Emil DuBrul, who essentially is as hardheaded, independent and zealous as Ethan Allen, but ethnically as different from him as Jacqueline Onassis is from Bess Truman.

Emil is probably in his forties, slight but wiry, with black hair and high color. He smiles easily, showing white teeth that contrast with his tanned skin. He is in perpetual motion but his movements are smooth and purposeful rather than nervous. He owns his farm and keeps a herd of fifty cows. He also has bought another farm and milks that herd as well. During the winter months he plows out driveways for about twenty families all the way from his farm into town. When there is no new snow, he chops wood for his sugarhouse, for his own use or to sell. From early March to April he taps his maple trees and boils sap, occasionally all night long. In other seasons he remodels his kitchen, re-papers the bedrooms, goes deer hunting or fishing, repairs all his own machinery and household equipment. He also drives his children eight miles into town so that they may attend the parochial school. I doubt if he knows or cares when his ancestors settled in Canada, but he would work right around the clock to earn the money for something he wanted. He is up at four, except in the snowy season when he often gets up at midnight to plow until chore time. I have never seen him angry, never heard him complain, even when his snowplow broke down when he had ten families still to plow out. He left the plow, went to town for the parts, mended it (in sub-zero weather with bare hands) and in half an hour waved as he drove out of the yard.

"Emil," I asked, "don't you ever stop?"

"Me? what should I do then? I never saw anyone dead from hard work, but I got no time to look for him," he laughed.

One winter we had a doctor from Vietnam visiting us. He had been in several American cities but was unfamiliar with rural American life. He had never touched a cow or seen one being milked, and was as delighted as a child with the milking machines on our neighbor's farm. He had also heard about maple syrup and wondered if the tapping process was similar to that used on the rubber plantations at home.

By luck, it was sugar weather in late March and it occurred to me that Emil was probably boiling his sap. I knew that

Emil welcomed visitors. Once I had taken a troop of twenty Brownies to watch him boiling. Although kindhearted, Emil never loses sight of the value of advertising. Several of the Brownies' mothers bought syrup.

We wallowed through the slush and mud in his barnyard and climbed the steep hill to his sugarhouse where the steam was billowing out in a white fragrant cloud. Emil was busy stuffing chunks of wood into the arch, stirring the syrup and pouring oil on the roaring fire.

I shouted an introduction and told him that Dr. Nguyen spoke French more easily than English.

"You speak French from the other side of the world," he called. "Me, I speak French from Vermont. The last time we saw Paris was never, eh?"

He explained how they tapped the trees, gathered the sap, boiled it down and drew off the syrup. As he spoke, in choppy phrases, he trotted to the end of the evaporator pan, poured a few drops of cream just before it foamed over, ran back to the storage tank, and back again to stoke the arch with more chunks of wood. He had been up most of the night tending the fire, had milked the cows, taken the children to school, cleaned the barns and now was back at the sugar house for another long stretch.

Dr. Nguyen shook his head and explained, "But you see in my country no one works like this. In the middle of the day it is hot. We do nothing for several hours."

Emil, incredulous, paused with his cream pitcher in mid-air. The heat from the fire and the steam from the pan were almost unbearable. Sweat was running into his eyes, his face was flushed and his shirt was plastered to his skin in dark blotches.

With a glistening straight face he looked at Dr. Nguyen. "Well, I don't know about that," he said. "You see I've never tried to work where it was hot."

17

A Vermont Year  **II**

Wary Season

A FEW years ago, I spent part of April in Florida. Having left our farmhouse still buttoned up in storm windows, with black-dotted snowdrifts cringing on the north side of stone walls, I was at first pleasantly lulled by the warmth and fragrance of Florida.

Wishing to be an appreciative visitor, I told a friendly young man how relaxing it was to step into a semi-tropical climate after the struggle for survival through a Vermont winter.

"Don't I know!" he exclaimed. "Why, one time I visited Vermont in the spring. Everyone had raved about how beautiful it was, and do you know what the shouting was about? Well, I'll tell you. It was pussywillows, a few crocuses, and some tree toads or something greatly overrated that you couldn't even hear unless you stopped talking."

He was right, of course. You can't hear spring come to Vermont unless you stop talking. And you can't see it unless you get out of your car and walk along a country road too high-crowned and muddy for driving.

The earliest signs are shy as a fawn. As you look across a field, you're not quite sure but you think it looks greener. There is a yellow glow along the twigs of the willows, and a haze of palest green softening the white birch tops. The succulent shoots of the skunk cabbage poke up boldly near the brooks, and ferns hunch their shoulders and uncurl. Along every roadside shad bush and choke cherries bloom in fairy delicacy. After remembered snow on upland meadows, it takes a second look to distinguish patches of bluets.

21

A Vermont Year

This wary season comes tentatively in our north country, slipping back into the woods to emerge again in a sunny hollow beyond the hemlocks. The redwing blackbirds creak as they house hunt through the pastures, and a meadowlark, swinging on the barbed-wire fence, gargles his melody, half reluctant to let his notes dissolve in the thin air. One evening when you step outdoors to bring in the sweet-smelling laundry (no longer frozen stiff in grotesque caricatures of the wearers) there is the eager insistent call of the peepers, still barely audible.

Perhaps the charm of a Vermont spring lies in the contrast to the long snowbound winter months when plunging to the barn through the snow proves so exhausting that you lean against the red clapboards to rest. No one who hasn't struggled in and out of socks, mittens, scarves, boots, jackets, and ski pants can know the elation of stepping outdoors with only a sweater tossed over the shoulders. And it would be as hard for me to feel the spirit of Easter unpreceded by winter as it would be to hang our Christmas ornaments on an avocado tree.

I can marvel at the orange tree producing blossoms, leaves and fruit simultaneously in the same way that I can admire the juggler keeping three balls in the air at once. But I am hushed with awe as I stand under an apple tree and look up through a cloud of pink and white caught in branches so recently bare.

Yes, you have to stop talking to hear spring come to Vermont, and you have to stop hurrying in order to see it. But, until you do, you haven't started living.

Summer in Vermont

THERE are a few folks between the Connecticut River and Lake Champlain and many outside the state boundaries, who will tell you that Vermont has no summer. That is true if summer means hurtling down into the steaming subways of New York, or driving bumper to bumper for three hours to a beach, and another itchy and sunburned three hours back to town at the end of the day.

It is also true if summer means day after day of motionless muggy air, with no more than a degree or two of change in the thermometer during the night.

But if summer means a high blue sky, the color of bluets at the horizon, and deep gentian blue overhead, you can find it in Vermont from the time the lilacs wilt on the graves, the day after Memorial Day, to the first curled and blackened pumpkin leaf in September. In fact, summer takes a few curtain calls after that first frost, returning in midday to blow a drowsy warm kiss as a promise that she'll be back for another season.

Summer is the combination of smells and sounds which tell of the muted activity in every meadow and hillside. It is the fragrance of sun-ripened strawberries and the popping sound as they are pulled from the plants.

It is the sweet perfume of red clover and the hum of the bees visiting from blossom to blossom. On the upland mowings or the flat meadows bordering the rivers, it is the fresh smell of new-mown hay and the click clack of the baler.

It is the scent of pink wild roses bowing beside every country road and the phoebe impatiently calling her mate to spell her on the nest in the woodshed.

No matter how warm the sun on your back, as you wrench loose from the blackberry bushes, the water of the brook has an icy sting to remind you that snow still lurks in a few crevasses in the mountains. It is the combination of looking back and reaching forward that makes our summers as irrational and charming as a girl.

It is no wonder that Vermonters have become known as cautious. They live always with seasons which are a memory of what has just been and the promise or threat of what is about to be.

The first spring flowers are all the more precious because snow may fall on them before morning. And the housewife turns gambler as she decides whether to gather in the wild riot of zinnias or risk leaving them out one more night in September. During haying season, every farmer watches the sky with anxiety and hustles in the last load before the storm.

For most of us, today is gathering up the stray ends of yesterday and trying to get a head start on tomorrow's stint. But now and then in summer, there is a day when the sky is so cloudless, and the sun so delicately warm that yesterday is forgotten, and tomorrow will certainly be another day.

And then, for a while, we can sit beside the waterfall, letting the cool water rush between our fingers without trying to stop it, letting the shadows lengthen without leaping up in dismay, and shutting out all awareness except the warm benediction of summer in Vermont.

Fall in Vermont

RIDING from O'Hare Airport to Evanston, Illinois, one day, I sat next to a girl returning to Northwestern from California. She asked where I came from and without thinking, I answered, "Vermont."

"Oh, I'd love to see Vermont in the fall," she exclaimed. "I've heard the trees turn lovely colors. What is it like?"

I realized quite suddenly that the memory of October in Vermont evokes much more than visual images. It was impossible for me to describe the look of fall without remembering the sound of my shoes scuffing through brittle leaves, and the smell of apples, bonfires and homemade ketchup simmering on the stove.

Oliver Wendell Holmes in *Autocrat of the Breakfast Table* said, "Memory, imagination, old sentiments and associations are more readily reached through the sense of smell than by almost any other channel."

During my four years in college, each year, on some previously unannounced morning in early October, the prolonged ringing of the chapel bell announced Mountain Day. Classes were canceled. The students were required—not that we needed such urging—to pack a picnic lunch in the dormitory kitchens and leave the campus to see the maples passing their torches up the hillsides through the pines.

As we sauntered along the lanes, picking purple asters and bittersweet, touching the marble smoothness of a pumpkin, smelling the woodsmoke from the farmhouses, we became aware of fall through senses that had not yet become atrophied in maturity. Even the most introspective mind unfolded a little in response to the clarion call of October.

It is impossible to walk through a tree tunnel of sugar maples, immersed in their golden light, even on a cloudy day, without absorbing courage from "the armour of light."

The first crimson sweep of swamp maple promises that soon a whole hillside will be ignited with scarlet and ochre. But memory of colors is elusive. We remember that the colors change and we can enjoy them in the present but we cannot recreate them through memory because the colors of fall, like flame, are ever-changing and quick to smolder into ash.

Much as I enjoy the sound of fall colors—amber, mahogany, persimmon, burnt umber and topaz—they do not evoke the memory of fall in Vermont. But at any time of the year, in Boston or Sioux Falls, when I open a jar of elderberry jelly, sniff a bushel basket of ripe tomatoes at a roadside stand, or press my nose into a bunch of asters in a florist shop, any one of these faint bittersweet fragrances opens the floodgates of memory and the colors "flash upon that inward eye" and I can see October in Vermont.

Winter in Vermont

THERE are mornings in Vermont when the red line of the thermometer sinks way down until it disappears into the round ball. Dramatic changes often occur during the night. Sometimes three or more inches of snow have fallen, rounding all the contours of the fields. Sometimes every twig and branch will be gleaming in its armor of ice, bending the birches down until they seem to be frozen waterfalls cascading into the wide pools of snow.

One night the temperature can drop from barely freezing at dusk to below zero early in the morning. Then not a branch stirs. But each twig on the lilac bushes at our windows has blossomed out with a ruffle of geometric-shaped frost crystals unlike the heavy clear sheath of ice that weighs down branches and fills the air with ominous crackling. These crystals are light and fragile. They seem to have burst out along each branch like tiny white flames frozen suddenly in the midst of their burning.

Winter in Vermont is like a great white cat, apparently asleep, with only its twitching tail tip warning that tense muscles are flexed under the white fur. It may snow for days softly, relentlessly, the sky so white that the falling flakes look gray against it. All the tracks of animals and people are gently erased, filled in and smoothed over for a fresh start.

When the snow has stopped falling, deep blue shadows in the vein-like pattern of birds' tracks will show where the blue jays fought over corn near the garage door. There will be a winding path of deeper tracks from the barn to the kitchen door, marking the trail which the cats have cautiously chosen. Boot marks will tell where I wobbled and slipped, where I dropped a mitten and splashed some water from the pail I was carrying to the chicken house. Out across the meadow a double ribbon of ski tracks will thread through the orchard and over the rocky ledge, now blasted half away by the construction of the interstate highway. A blanket of snow has covered it, returning it, if only in illusion, to the broad white fields. But now there is no sign of life and no motion but the silent downward sifting of the snow. Tomorrow these fields will be crisscrossed and pocked by the struggles of hungry, searching, hunting animals and people. But today all the old scars are filled in, the sharp rocks are marshmallows, and the curtain of falling snow is still lowered in front of the empty stage that waits for tomorrow's drama.

Fauna & Flora

Pruning Time

IT seemed as though we never would get the hang of pruning those apple trees. Along about sugaring time, when fringes of speckled snow still edged the northern side of fences, we would walk across the spongy fields to our orchard. It wasn't an orchard really, just one pear and six apple trees. We didn't know who had planted them. We knew who lived in the house one hundred and fifty years ago and they told us a good deal about their life in the diaries we found between the floor joists of the attic. But these trees weren't more than forty years old. So it was another couple who decided which varieties to plant. They chose two McIntosh, the first to ripen, their skins turning almost purple-red, rubbed to a high crimson sheen on your shirt front. The juice spurted out of these and the flesh was white, with tiny red veins. Those were for eating apples, for school lunch pails, and rosy sauce if cooked with the skins on. I think the woman insisted on two Northern Spies for pies. Knobby, red-streaked, they grew so big that four would make a pie. Of course the juice jellied and stuck to the pan but the flavor made you forget that. Then thrift probably prompted them to plant two Baldwins, good winter keepers, hard as rocks and ripening long after the deer had eaten the windfalls under the other trees.

When we bought the farm, these trees had been neglected for a long time. They were a mass of bloom in the spring but the branches were tangled and the fruit small and wormy. We tried to prune them the first year. We read how to do it and studied diagrams. But every apple tree looks different

33

and none like the ones in the pictures. We were fearful of cutting live branches. I think we thought it might kill the tree. But between the pruning and spraying and the fact that the next year was a good apple year anyway, the trees throve. In September the branches were bowed nearly to the ground with large sound fruit.

Of course I don't say our pruning was correct. It just seemed to come more easily after that. You stand under a tree and look up through the bare branches at the sky. You see the dead branches first because their buds are not swollen. After these are out, you'll see limbs that cross each other and rub the wrong way. Then there are weak crotches that would not be able to support the weight of heavy fruit. The water sprouts don't get anywhere, in spite of their vigor, so off they come, and soon the tree has a cup-like shape, open to the sky in the middle, able to receive the sunlight and rain and produce something worthwhile.

I don't know just when we came to have the knack of it. It's something two people don't quite understand one day, and then comes a day when they seem to have always known.

Lambs and Wolfs

WE didn't really mean to have sheep, and I'm sure no thoughtful sheep would ever mean to have us. But then, I've never known a thoughtful sheep. They just look that way.

Contrary to the logic of the nursery rhyme, I don't believe that the lamb loved Mary because "Mary loved the lamb, you know." The lamb tagged at her heels because she fed him. From our undistinguished experience as shepherds, we have learned that a bottle-fed lamb will shadow you like crazy, but the one nursed by the ewe will tag the ewe and regard humans with cold expressionless eyes that have no lustre of love.

Sheep and Wolfs got together quite by chance on a perfectly beautiful May day when the girls and I were on our way to visit my sister in Weston, Vermont. If George had been along we would have driven directly to Weston by the shortest route. He's a no-nonsense sort of traveler who likes to relax after he reaches his destination and not on the way. The girls have inherited (or been browbeaten into) my fondness for side trips, meandering and acquiring variegated flora and fauna along the way. I think I developed this habit as a child when the annual journey from Montclair, New Jersey to Maine took three days. This was from necessity, not choice. We always had at least one flat tire a day, and frequent combustion problems beneath the hood. While the tire was being patched and pumped up by hand, I gathered bouquets of wild violets or asters, depending on whether the trip was north in June or south in September, and so many rocks that it was not by chance that the tire which gasped its last was usually the one under my corner. I still like to do this. All the girls need to do is mention a nearby marble quarry and my foot is on the brake and my fingers itching for scraps of marble. Our garage bulges with mounds of these souvenirs, totally ignored since the day of their acquisition. According to my husband an equally large collection of rocks can be found in my head.

No marble quarries lured us that fine May afternoon. Our digression was to visit the Morgan horse farm near Middlebury. We wanted to see the mares and foals together in the field. But there were disappointingly few at that time, and we decided to go on to the nearby sheep farm to see the lambs.

I've heard sheep calling back and forth on the misty hillsides of Grasmere, but nothing had prepared us for the rollicking sound and sight of more than fifty ewes and lambs gamboling and bleating in the lush green pasture. One little lamb trotted along the fence, pressing its snub nose through the bars and baa-ing with startling volume and imperativeness. The shepherd's wife told us that its mother had died and that she had to bottle-feed the lamb four times a day. She hinted that this was a nuisance and she wished that someone would adopt the lamb. The girls looked at me and I at them and we shouted in unison, "We'll take her."

After an hour's wait for official permission, we finally were off with Lambie skidding about stiff-legged in the back of the Jeep station wagon whenever the girls let go of her for an instant. The next stop was at a drugstore in Middlebury for a large black nipple and a baby bottle.

It was almost dark when we reached my sister's house and fell out of the car in our eagerness to display Lambie. The greeting was too much for the lamb who catapulted out of Patty's arms and took to the woods. We chased her in a panic that we might lose her in the increasing dark. She bounced vertically and horizontally in a panic that we might not. We were all exhausted when she was finally tackled and carried into the garage. George joined us after supper and fortunately was as delighted as we were with Lambie.

There is no creature that sheds its charm with maturity more than a sheep, and when I think of what a stupid, ungainly sheep Lambie became, it is hard to remember her appealing little face, her tightly curled white fleece several sizes too big for her, her enormous knees and fringed hooves and gait like a child walking in his father's shoes. She looked like an Easter card, felt like a baby's toy, and sounded like the Chicago stockyards. During the long ride home that night, nine-year-old Patty sat on the bare station wagon floor holding Lambie on her lap for one hundred miles. George and I smiled at each other, congratulating ourselves on the devotion and tenderness of our child, until Patty straightened us out.

"I'm not holding her to make her happy. It's the only way she'll shut up, and the noise drives me nuts!"

For three days everyone fought for the opportunity to feed Lambie her bottle. For the following two months, until she was weaned, everyone fought to avoid it. It was great fun, at first, to run across the yard and have Lambie follow you leaping and bounding like a Walt Disney lamb. But very soon she became full grown, earth bound, and dull.

After she was bred, there was a revival of interest in her at the time her lamb was due. Unfortunately her lamb came early on a very cold night in March and we found the stiff, wet little thing dead on the cement floor. The next year, we provided her with a better pen and lots of hay, and hovered over her as soon as she began to paw around making a nest. When she dropped her lamb, we were so afraid he might become chilled that we brought hay into our cellar with Lambie, the new lamb and a roll of snow fence. This made Lambie nervous and unwilling to nurse the lamb. That made me nervous and unwilling to leave them alone, so I climbed into the improvised pen and spent an hour trying to connect the lamb with the dairy. That made me allergic to hay, lamb dander, or unmaternal ewes, and I staggered up the cellar stairs with my eyes and nose streaming and my face swollen.

Jackie (so named because he was born during the Jackie Gleason television program) throve and surpassed his mother in stupidity, dirtiness and strength. He enjoyed butting, first his mother, then the rest of us. It was all very funny when he weighed fifteen pounds and felt like a soft pillow, but when he weighed seventy-five pounds and would catch you right behind the knees or in the seat of the pants when you bent over to transplant tomato plants, the humor was lost on the buttee.

During the winter, when the snow drifted against the sheep fence, Jackie found he could climb on a snow bank and jump over the fence. As the snow melted, Jackie compensated by jumping higher each day and maintaining his freedom. Lambie, Heidi (a beautiful rose-pink lamb, who wasn't really pink but had acquired the shade by rubbing against a red snow fence) and Jackie's younger sister, Merrilee, followed him over the barriers.

Our lawn looked like an English park, briefly. Jackie destroyed the bucolic illusion by cropping the fat buds from every tulip while curling his lip in disgust at the grass. We tried tying him. We got higher and stronger fence and ruined our knuckles, dispositions, and Saturday afternoons trying to make a Jackie-proof enclosure. But he won, at least temporarily.

With Jackie, Lambie, Merrilee and Heidi corralled in the

barn, we held a council of war. It was either the gardens or the sheep. We expected protests from the girls but fate had kindly tipped the scales. Only a few days before, with Lambie in the back of the truck, and Patty in the cab with me, the engine had gone dead when we were halfway across the highway near the school. Several of Patty's classmates were walking home from school and gathered to watch. Cars honked, children shouted, and Lambie baaed in fine voice. Patty shrunk farther and farther down on the front seat. When one sophisticated boy shouted, "They're taking the sheep to be married," Patty's ignominy knew no bounds. So when the question of parting with the sheep arose, Patty wished them Godspeed with unusual warmth.

The sheep were loaded into the truck, the tail gate fastened, and the crunch of gravel would have drowned out any sad farewells. But there weren't any. Everyone was waving happily at the white muzzles thrust over the tailgate and there was not a wet eye in the family.

Thumbs Down (Green Ones)

PEOPLE who claim to have green thumbs should wear mittens, sit on their hands, or admire their abnormality by the light of the moon when the rest of us hoers of the weeds are trying to relax our back muscles.

It isn't the sight of a green thumb that is so disturbing. They are rarely displayed except on rubber gardening gloves at the hardware store. It is the missionary zeal of anyone who feels that Ceres endowed him with divine insight into a plant's psyche. It is as pompous for a home gardener to feel that he produced the plants as it would be for an obstetrician to claim that he made the baby.

Our garden grows in spite of us, in the same way that our children have turned into charming people in spite of the traumatic experience of living with us during their formative years.

Of course a garden doesn't plant itself, although the dill and tomato volunteers make a good try each year. But it can't plant itself in rows properly spaced to allow room for the rototiller to cultivate between them. (According to my husband, neither can I, but next year. . . .)

A prevalent illusion is that we have a free choice in the amount and variety of seeds we select. We're wrong. From the time the first seed catalogue brightens the coffee table in January until you mulch the rose bushes in the fall, you are under the influence of alchemists.

The best thing to do is to grab your hoe and man your battle station in the garden because, between the forces of nature and the pressure of green thumbs, the conflicts in

40

your patch will accelerate so rapidly that you will have to fight to enjoy the growing season.

In the first place, if you pay any attention to the suggestions for the size of a garden suitable for a family of four, you are doomed to such drab winter chores as throwing out onions that have started to sprout and carrying out moldy pumpkins that should have been changed into Cinderella's coach. I'd just like to see that suggested family of four (giants, all of them) with the appetites of Dispos-Alls and special cravings for kale and turnips.

There is no cure for the disease of planting too much. It recurs every May, but the ensuing depression is relieved in our case by raising chickens who eat the surplus. Even after we've given corn and tomatoes to every neighbor to whom we are in debt for taxiing the children, sold the Indian ornamental corn to the florist, and pressed a pumpkin upon every child of jack-o'-lantern age, and even after I've dried little bunches of parsley, filled the freezer with asparagus, peas and broccoli, and canned and pickled the peppers and tomatoes, we still have vegetables left over for the chickens.

But who among us has moral fibre sturdy enough to plant only one hill of summer squash or a single foot of parsley when the amount of seeds in the tiny parsley packet will give you a hedge ten feet long? Each September we vow that we will be sensible the next year, but even as we speak these words we know that they are as hollow as promises made during a hangover.

Next, you must restrain your impulse to plant all the beans or radishes at the same time. Save some seed for successive plantings. We do, and the beans planted May 15, May 30 and June 15 all mature at the same date. The coöperative little radishes mature on schedule, but we haven't eaten the first crop before the second is ready, and by the time the third crop matures each member of the family admits that he doesn't really like radishes anyway. They make him burp.

Another attack from the self-styled green thumbers will be upon your inadequate insect control. Very simple, they tell you. All you do is arm yourself with Chlordane for Japanese beetles, Lindane for woolly aphids, Methoxychlor for Mexican beetles, a fungicide such as Captan, and who would dream of being without Dithane z78 for downy mildew on cucurbits, and some soil fumigants such as Oxyquinoline and Chloropicrin?

I'm sure they're all dandy, but inasmuch as our medicine cabinet (and my husband a doctor) contains a thermometer, aspirin, and a bottle of hardened nail polish which I keep forgetting to throw out, why should we confuse our vegetables with chemotherapy and sail through pill-less days ourselves? I know there are people who take uppers to counteract their downers. Maybe this makes them strong enough to carry all those preparations out to their gardens. In the time it takes to read one label, with no thought at all of understanding it, I can knock off all the potato bugs into a soup can of kerosene. We do shake one all-purpose powder on the cabbage family to discourage those little green worms, and on the cucumbers to scare off the striped beetles. The rest of the insects in our garden are literally for the birds. I'll help, up to a point, but when a few of those huge green worms start denuding the tomato plants, I think I smell something burning on the stove.

At last the beans are in blossom. The drowsy hum of the bees and the mellow warmth of the sun indicate a short siesta under the apple tree. But no sooner have you shaken the pebbles out of your sneakers when along comes your green thumb friend who doesn't approve of your apple tree. You know why not? Because it should be espaliered against the garage wall in the angular stance of that Hindu god with four sets of arms. As if this weren't torment enough for one tree, you really should graft it so that lower left branch one will produce two Greenings while upper branch three will bear four perfect Winesaps.

I like our apple trees to look relaxed. I like to pick a Northern Spy off the Spy tree and a Mac from the little Mac next to it.

I'll admit that since we pruned and sprayed the orchard, we now have fruit that resembles apples. That's an improvement and I'll go along with man's interference to that extent, but I prefer hedges that look like hedges rather than carved roosters, and I like apple trees to look as though a small boy could climb into the top branches or skin the cat on the lower ones. You can't skin the cat on the left lower one of an espaliered tree.

If I voice these opinions I am told (if I'm still included in the conversation) that I am motivated by a functional rather than an ornamental goal. You just bet your muddy garden boots I am! To be specific, what motivates me is the taste of the first peas popped out of their crisp dewy pods only minutes before they are popped into my mouth. The thought of the tender young ears of corn, dropped into boiling water for no more than five minutes, and glistening with butter, turns me into a weeding wonder. The memory of a melon so fragrant that you could locate it with your eyes closed, or salads made from six varieties of lettuce, a few small leaves of spinach, and a chopped scallion, lightly tossed with homemade dressing motivates my ten thumbs into clinging to the vibrating handles of the rototiller as we hurtle noisily between rows.

I'm not blind to the beauty in our garden. The variety of greens from the blue-green of the pea vines with their pewter finish to the delicate chartreuse of the first corn blades satisfies my soul as much as their fruits satisfy my stomach. A few minutes in the early morning spent cutting the asparagus tips and marveling at the shading from amethyst to jade is tranquilizer enough to sustain me through an eight-year-old's birthday party.

I'm just fed up with those people who admire their green thumbs. Why, they know all the answers before I've asked a question. And there is a question that has been on my mind. Do you know a good dermatologist? I seem to have a fascinating discoloration. Just a minute, I'll take off my gloves and show you!

Move Me, Move My Menagerie

TO live in the country and work in the city is a dream to which our family does not have exclusive rights. The only unusual aspect about our dream is that it came true as soon as we moved to Vermont.

Because we have the space and inclination, we keep pigs, chickens, turkeys, a horse, and a varying census of cats. We have also, on occasion, been so mesmerized by day-old ducklings, cosset lambs, a baby kid, small rabbits or a puppy, that we have passed through phases of catering to all of them. The usual June roll call, however, includes two adult humans, two daughters, one horse, two pigs, fifty laying hens, one hundred young chickens, twelve six-week-old turkey poults, two old male cats, one mother cat, and about three or four kittens. When these are distributed over ninety-two acres, and in and out of two large barns and a chicken house, there is no crowding. In fact this farm could easily support twenty or thirty cows. The farm could, but the farmer's wife won't, because the farmer works in town and the daily chores must be done by the farmer's wife—me.

Idyllic as this may sound, and smoothly as it runs most of the time (I've not forgotten how I plunged through drifts of snow to the barn with two heavy pails of water, when the temperature was twenty below), the whole menage is thrown into turmoil each June when we "move to the country."

You see, before we dreamed that we would ever live year-round in Vermont, we had bought the little hillside rockery in Jericho Center to which we rushed from New York each spring so that our children could pick violets, buttercups, Indian paintbrush and goldenrod until mid-September, when they would return to Central Park to pick cigar bands and gum wrappers.

Now, a more sensible family would have kept the farm in Jericho for summer use, and bought an ugly old inexpensive house, or a pretty new expensive house in Burlington. Not we! Instead we bought the wonderful one-hundred-and-fifty-year-old farmhouse three miles out of town.

That, of course, meant that we could keep our animals all year round and move them with us from South Burlington to Jericho in June and back again in September.

That first fall, the pigs were taken straight from Jericho to the slaughterhouse. That meant that all we had to move, in the way of livestock, was about sixty laying hens and a few cats. In the light of subsequent experiences it seems like nothing at all. All you do is put the hens in crates, put the crates in the Jeep station wagon, put the cats and people in front and start the car. But it rained that day. Not only that day. It had been raining for many days. The chicken yard was a chocolate fudge morass with a very unchocolately odor. While George and I skidded and sloshed in pursuit of the hens, the little girls were supposed to round up the cats. Debbie, who usually wore one of the kittens tucked into the elastic waist band of her shorts, tried to squeeze the kittens into a bushel basket as Patty brought them to her. Every time Debbie lifted the lid to admit a cat, the one she had just put in scrambled out. This resulted in a lot of name-calling on both sides and eventual scratches from the kittens and tears from the pig-tailed set.

Meanwhile, George and I were filling the crates with bedraggled, protesting hens who were mad as guess what. Generous dollops of mud spattered on my face and George's shirt, and were plastered solidly as far up as elbows and knees. When the crates were shoved into the Jeep, the kittens finally secured in a grain bag, and some of the thicker mud scraped off, we were on our way to South Burlington.

The rain had stopped by the time we got there. The mud was drying and scaling off us like sycamore bark. We carried the crates to the chicken house and opened them. Judging from the hens' reaction when we stuffed them into the crates we thought they'd be just dying to hop out. They wouldn't budge. We had to pry and pull out every last squawking fowl. When the last one was daintily stepping about the chicken house, we shut the door and went back to the house. I seemed to hear knocking on the front door. My boots were too muddy to wear indoors, so I kicked them off and walked into the kitchen in my none too clean bare feet. The knocking persisted. I thought the children were being funny and "coming to call." With a good deal of irritation, I marched through the hall shouting, "For Gosh sakes, if you want to come, come in the back!"

I flung the door open, but instead of two grubby pig-tailed blonds at waist height, there stood one of the deans at the University and his lady.

Temporary paralysis of the larynx was general. The lady extended a white-gloved hand which she withdrew involuntarily at the sight of my filthy claw. The sound of George scuttling upstairs to hide loosened my vocal chords and wrath. I wasn't going to be left in this predicament while he sneaked a shower.

"George," I called. "Dr. and Mrs. Camp are here."

George dragged back down the stairs and managed a brave smile after an eloquent glare in my direction.

"Come in," we urged, without enthusiasm. They did, with the greatest reluctance and seated themselves on the edge of

47

two chairs as near to the door as possible. George snatched a newspaper to sit on, and I sat on my hands and wished there were some way to hide my large and muddy feet.

Mrs. Camp drew a wisp of white lace handkerchief from her bag and slyly managed to get her nose covered.

"We'd love to meet your sweet little girls," she murmured through the mask.

Now our little girls were, at that age, about as sweet and sour as most. Ordinarily they greeted guests shyly but at least civilly. But this day had been trying. Lack of food and an abundance of scratches had worn the sweetness pretty thin. I knew what they looked like and hoped they had gone out to explore the barn. But with that unerring gift for being absent when wanted, and present when unwanted, the two "sweet little girls" hurtled into the room, hair hanging in lank wisps over their tear-stained muddy faces.

"Who are they?" Patty snarled, pointing a dirty finger at the Camps. Debbie simpered and crawled under the table.

Explanation fell flat. In a very few minutes, with polite remarks to the effect that country living must be wonderful *if* you like it, they picked their way with gathering momentum to the door.

We see them occasionally at University dinners. I always wear shoes, but they have never returned.

Of course that was the first hegira and now, years later, you'd expect that experience would have led to efficiency. Well, you can expect it, if you like, but the fact remains that when you are dealing with animals, anything can happen, and in our case it usually does.

Take the horse, for instance. I've secretly wished someone would for a long time, even though I was the one who pleaded her cause at the beginning. Lots of people transport horses here and there in trucks. We've had Lady three years.

48

Move Me, Move My Menagerie

Fortunately, we've had our truck three years too, because Lady couldn't fit into a Jeep station wagon if she wanted to. She can just fit in our red half-ton truck, but she doesn't want to. In the first place, she's very temperamental about being caught just to be ridden. But her horse sense became a kind of premonition of doom when the day came first to move Lady to Jericho. She teased us into false hope by being perfectly willing on that day to be bridled. We backed the truck to an elevated spot which reduced the angle of the ramp. We even camouflaged the ramp with hay and put some oats in the truck. But Lady clamped her yellow teeth firmly on the bit and became a statue. A light slap on the flank was ruled ineffective after her hind hooves grazed George's ear. Pulling on the bridle became a tug of war. It was obvious that the only thing about to give was the bridle. Finally Patty, who was still living in a dream world of television horses who count to four and untie knots, got on Lady, rode her around a bit and then rode quickly up the ramp and into the truck from which height she and the horse regarded her open-mouthed parents with understandable scorn.

Oh, well, over a period of seven years, or fourteen trips, there must have been one trip when everything went smoothly. I can't seem to remember it though. We counted ourselves lucky when nothing more was lost than tempers though the seventeen-mile trip takes only twenty-five minutes on the road, our cocker spaniel found that long enough to produce carsickness. The sheep peered through the sideboards of the truck with their pale eyes and baaed continuously. The pigs, if small, were put into grain bags where they writhed and screamed and frequently worked their way loose. The cats moaned in misery, and when young, the children often joined in the common lament. When they were older, the girls merely ducked their heads below the

49

dashboard until we were well beyond possible recognition by classmates. But I remember one trip when Patty was stationed in the back of the Jeep to stand guard over a crate of ducks, a sheep, two bags of pigs and a carton of cats. I was driving, but in the rear-view mirror I could see Patty's mouth opening and shutting spasmodically and undoubtedly producing great wails which were completely drowned out by the cacophony of quacks, baas, miaows and shrieks.

I once knew a cat who loved to ride in cars. In fact she made a habit of leaping into any car parked in her driveway and then lay quietly in wait until the driver had gone a half mile or so. I suspect she found it exhilarating to pounce on the unsuspecting driver's neck. The driver found it more than that. But none of our cats has ever shown anything but loathing for cars. We finally became convinced that no trip was tolerable unless the cats were boxed, bagged or basketed. A basket gives the cat more air and a better view but also the opportunity to take a swipe at you with a claw if you are foolish enough to make friendly advances. Mitty, the progenitor of a long line of black Mitties with white paws, was the first adult cat to take the trip. She was such a friendly, dignified cat, so tolerant of the many abuses of a cat-loving family that it never occurred to us that she wouldn't sit quietly beside me on the front seat.

Moving day that year was hot and sultry. For some reason, the children were with George in the "soft" car, and I had the simple task of driving the crated chickens and one cat. Before we were up our driveway, Mitty became restless. She began to moan and sway back and forth. Her first flying leap toward the partly open window brought me over to the side of the road to wind up all the windows and pat the cat. As soon as we were off again, the tip of her tail began to twitch ominously and the banshee wails resumed. It was stifling in the closed chicken-scented car. My shirt stuck alternately to me and the back of the seat. For seventeen miles Mitty leaped, crouched, and sprang from the back of my neck to the top of the crates. She could have walked the distance with less expenditure of energy. So could I. When we finally drew into the yard at Jericho and opened the door, I fell out onto the cool grass, and Mitty shot over my head and streaked off behind the barn. In a short while I dried off and calmed down, but Mitty didn't resume family relations for two days.

At least Mitty and I didn't involve anyone besides ourselves in our misery; not directly, that is. I am sure that anyone in a car behind us on the highway gripped his wheel and allowed us a few more lengths between cars whenever Mitty catapulted from front to rear. But no one was asked for or volunteered aid.

On another trip we had a volunteer. It was one of the first trips from South Burlington to Jericho in June, and Patty, as the older child, was in charge of the noisy menagerie in the Jeep. She had no particular trouble with the boxed ducklings or the basketed cat, but there were two young pigs, each tied up in an old grain bag. There were a certain number of holes in the bags which we kindly thought would provide ventilation. The pigs thought the holes could provide escape as well, and wasted no time in enlarging them. For a few miles Patty was able to shove the snouts back in when they protruded, but when one pig got his head, shoulders and one front leg out, Patty added her shrieks to his, and I had to pull over to the side of the road. Far across a field, a man was hoeing. I saw him straighten up and look in our direction. Whatever way the wind was blowing, he would have had to be deaf not to hear the shrieking of two young pigs and Patty's cries of, "Help me! Help me!"

51

Fauna & Flora

I had just managed to shove the pig back in the bag and retie the fragments when the farmer's face, flushed and horrified, was thrust over the tailgate.

"What's in that bag?" he gasped, waving his hoe menacingly.

"A pig," I replied meekly. "It was getting out and—"

"Well Jeesum," he panted. "You gave me a turn. I thought —all that screaming—well, pigs do sound kinda human!"

It didn't seem funny to me until we were several miles down the road. In fact I carefully avoided that road until we had turned in the Jeep for an entirely different-looking car.

The Berry Pickers

THEIR natural habitat during the summer months is among the thickets bordering the dirt roads of northern New England, though they may also be found at the edge of woodlands and in overgrown pastures. It is difficult to distinguish the male from the female, except that he is slightly longer in the body, while the female tends to be plumper in the mid-portions. The plumage of those indigenous to the area is usually faded blue below with white or khaki across the back, while the migratory species may flaunt brilliant colors interspersed with patches of bare skin. The prudent ones may be identified by their long pants and long-sleeved shirts, but a prudent berry picker is almost as rare as the American eagle and even more predatory.

They are unable to read signs saying, "Warning! Test firing!," "No Trespassing," or "High Voltage Wires." They cannot hear the bellow of a Jersey bull, the wailing of their own young, or the impatient horn-honking produced by their mates.

I know. I am one of them, and though I write this in the early spring when the berry bushes are scarcely leafed out, I can see the handwriting on the wall. I know that one soft summer day, when the children are absolute angels, or better yet, visiting friends, and when time does not have to be torn off in small chunks, I will find myself staring with glazed eyes at the leaning tower of berry baskets in the back hall. There are other favored containers. My father was partial to honey pails for berrying. He believed that the hand that holds the pail can remain relatively available for pulling down a thorny branch or maintaining balance in a tricky spot. But we don't buy honey in pails. Out of the nebulae of childhood memories, I seem to remember blueberrying with a small milk can, pewter colored, with a pouring lip and a metal top that fitted down inside. This type of container would have advantages for the very young.

The gathering of the berry pickers is not arranged. It just evolves. My experience is limited, but in every family of my acquaintance there are divided camps on the subject of berry picking. You either are a berry picker or you aren't. You either hate it or are enslaved by it. Weather warnings, threats or rewards won't budge a member of either camp across the dividing line.

My husband is not a berry picker. In the first place, he doesn't even like blackberries or raspberries. The seeds get in his teeth, well, not in them, between them. He likes strawberries and blueberries but only when they appear as a *fait accompli*, such as a shortcake or pie. The preliminary encounter between pickers and prickers holds no fascination for him whatever. I have long since abandoned the hope that he might like to come along for the ride or walk, depending on our destination. He not only wouldn't, but the one time he was persuaded to join us against his will, the whole enterprise had a diabolical effect on his personality.

As soon as the pickers had scattered among the bushes, he started the car and drove down the road a few hundred yards, trying to make us believe he had gone off without us. When this had no effect, he began tossing pebbles into the bushes at safe but startling distances. He commented loudly on the imminence of a thunderstorm and the suitability of the terrain for snakes. I am quite sure that he stopped short of a tantrum only because the picking proved so poor that day that we gave up reluctantly and agreed to go home.

54

The Berry Pickers

But he is not the only one in the resistant camp. Our younger daughter prefers almost any activity to berrying. When she was small, however, the thought of staying home alone seemed even more distasteful. She would tag along, removing and losing her sneakers at intervals. She would carry a tiny basket and trudge up the hill, through the old sugar bush where the summer foliage made a dappled pattern of green and gold on her small blond head. But the basket was pure affectation. She was never known to deposit berries anywhere but in her mouth. In fact, after the first few, she abandoned picking them even to eat, and resorted to swinging on the young maples, making boats out of the leaves and stems, or getting her jersey shirt impaled on a thorny bush.

Our older daughter, however, inherited the berry-picking chromosome from me, as I did from my father, and she is as unable to free herself from its power as she would be to change the color of her eyes.

The behavior pattern of the berry picker is familiar to every bearer of the purple stain. When a berry picker walks down a country road, his eyes dart here and there evaluating the terrain in terms of berries. He rarely suggests a berrying expedition. Oddly enough it is the eaters, rather than the pickers, who instigate that sort of thing. The berry picker, in fact, is apt to keep busy at other tasks and avoid mentioning the ripening fruit (of which he is acutely aware) in the same way that an alcoholic avoids a cocktail party. And for the same reason. One berry softly plopped into the basket and he is driven to take another and another. The true addict rarely eats any berries while he picks. He hoards them. The vines reach out and rake his shirt and skin, but he is under temporary anesthesia.

One of the irritating habits of the berry picker is his practice of displaying the livid network of scratches on his wrists and ankles to all non-berry-pickers, after he has regained consciousness. He is as surprised and gratified by his wounds as a skier is by a fractured leg on the last day of spring skiing.

But while he may be oblivious to the discomforts of berrying, and apparently preoccupied only with the next bush (which surely is laden with the largest and juiciest berries) his other senses are acutely receptive to surrounding stimuli. He hears the drone of the bees and the insistent higher shrill of the cicadas, punctuated by the cawing of one huge sentinel crow at the top of a dead pine tree. He is nourished by the fragrance of milkweed and red clover, heavy sweet summer smells, with all the mellowness of a ripened season. He remembers tiny bluets and wild violets of early spring, but theirs was a crisp cold fragrance reminiscent of the snow still dampening the earth at their roots. The fragrance of summer is warm and round and full of nectar.

It is this subtle hypnotism of pleasant sensations that lures the berry pickers off over the stone walls, up through the grove of old maples, or back into the hills on old abandoned lumber roads. Like the children of Hamelin, they are deaf to the voices of their families, insensible to pain, and unaware of time or responsibility, drawn by a melody unheard by others ears to a rendezvous they are impelled to keep.

Michael the Goat

※※

MOST young animals lose some of their exuberance on the way to maturity. Baby pigs are whirling dervishes compared to a lethargic sow. High-tailed kittens gradually stop pouncing and settle down to a career of contemplation and grooming. These animals become less volatile and unpredictable. The goat, apparently, operates in reverse.

Michael was a snow-white six-week-old kid when we bought him for the exorbitant fee of ten dollars. His skin was obviously too big for him, as were also his knees and hooves. He followed us around with stiff uncertain steps and baaed piteously if left too far behind. But as time strengthened his legs, and many bottles of milk smoothed his skin, he became the most irrational and unpredictable member of a household not noted for its dearth of these characteristics.

At two months, Michael pulled the clothes off the line before I could rush, screaming, out of the house. If he had done this regularly, even the most stupid housewife would have hung the clothes higher or indoors, or used the clothesline to tether the goat. But for days Michael would graze peacefully beneath the billowing sheets and flapping shirttails with complete disinterest. Then, suddenly, his lust for laundry would be reactivated. So it became necessary to tie Michael up. Goat folklore to the contrary, our goat never ate the clothes, or tin cans, or anything except grass, grain, or buttercups, but he mouthed and pulled at everything within sight of his mild, unexpressive eyes.

Each morning he was untied and led to the spring to drink. It never was that simple. As you struggled to untie his rope, Michael would jerk and lunge, pulling the knot tighter. So you would loop the rope around your foot, leaving a bit of slack to help make the untying easier. That was all right until Michael gave a convulsive lunge, snapping the rope tight enough around your foot to leave a red welt. If you were so foolhardy as to turn your back upon him and bend over the knot, Michael would eye you sidewise, rear back and charge, butting you head first into the knot, the fence, and also a fine frenzy.

When the rope was finally untied, Michael dashed for the spring, dragging you stumbling and plunging after him down the rocky hillside. But if you leaned back on the rope, he might suddenly stop to eat a buttercup, sending you sprawling over his back, flat on your face in the meadow.

All in all, Michael became so strong and difficult to handle, and the members of the family became so gay with bruises, that we decided to take him to the local vet for advice on removal of his horns or hormones.

This involved a four-mile ride to the village of Richmond, so Michael was stuffed into the back of the Jeep station wagon, the children in the front, the kittens thrown out, my handbag thrown in (all repeated several times in different order) and then we took off.

Not being familiar with vet's fees, I decided to cash a check and parked in front of the bank, diagonally headed toward the curb, as was the custom in the village. The children and I went into the bank; Michael, complaining loudly, was left in the station wagon. I was tucking away my money and picking up handfuls of deposit slips which Debbie had been strewing around the floor, when a car horn began honking steadily, as though stuck. I glanced through the window and realized with dismay that it was the horn of our car. Michael had leaped into the driver's seat and, finding

the position squeezy, was jammed against the horn. His kicking hind legs released the emergency brake and the car, with Michael at the wheel, rolled slowly towards the curb. The population of Richmond is not large, but a good per cent of it stood around the car in evident enjoyment while I pushed my way through and most unwillingly claimed ownership.

Michael was heaved into the back. The "raisins" were brushed off the seat and we managed the two blocks to the vet's without incident.

There was no sign on the house but I had been told that it was the white frame house with a porch, so Michael and I and the two little girls leapt up the steps and rang the bell. I saw with horror that Michael had just made a puddle on the grass rug and was now sprinkling the area with "raisins."

Handing the rope to Patty, I began to mop and whisk with Kleenex until Patty shrieked, "Mommy, he's eating their shrubbery!"

The shrubbery was a row of choice tuberous begonias in pots, which Michael had deflowered and was now savoring with closed eyes.

I grabbed the rope and fled from the porch, dragging the reluctant goat and protesting children after me. A neighbor opened her window in the house next door and called out, "If you was looking for the vet, that's two houses over."

I wasn't looking for the vet any longer. I was looking for a nice big black chasm that would open at our feet and drop us into oblivion. The next best thing was the car and speedy retreat.

In June, when Michael had first come to us, I had wondered how we would ever be able to bear to part with him, even in death. By Labor Day, I couldn't wait.

Fauna & Flora

As my husband drove off with Michael to the animal auction, both of them eyeing me reproachfully, my heart was filled with joy. I waved them off, light of heart, and went leisurely to hang out the laundry on a brand new clothesline.

Cats Always, or Do They?

THE next time a guest remarks, "The thing I don't like about cats is that they always . . . ," I am not going to push the cat out of the door and apologize to the friend. I am going to push the friend outside and apologize to the cat.

Over a period of twelve years we have claimed and been tolerated by nearly fifty cats. The census varies, of course, from one to an all-time high of eighteen at once. We never intended to have eighteen cats. It is simply that cats are prolific, and we are too weak willed to do away with kittens. By the time they are full grown, and in some cases less charming, the four members of our family can never agree on which cats are expendable. Their variable behavior makes the expression "cats always" begin to weaken.

There are some attributes that cats *almost* always have. They are nearly always capable and devoted mothers whether the litter is the first or the tenth. They are almost always hungry, and almost always growl over meat even when they are too tiny to tear it apart. But to say that they are always sneaky or loyal, vicious or tolerant, is about as risky as proclaiming, "My son would never do that!"

We have had cats who preferred to be indoors and who adapted to human standards for indoor behavior with satisfaction to both parties. We have had others who were unbearable in the house, leaping onto tables, scratching the furniture, and pacing restlessly at the door. One mother cat chose a doll carriage in our little girls' playroom as the place to have her kittens, while another dug a long tunnel through the hay to the remotest corner of the barn for a nest. Some have led us to their babies, and some invented elaborate ruses to throw us off the track.

Folklore to the contrary, none of our male cats has ever attacked a kitten. In fact they are more likely to retreat in apparent fear of the young, a phenomenon observable among some human fathers. Mr. Cat, a dignified gentleman, eats anything he catches in the field on the spot. Mrs. Cat makes a habit of bringing back her hunting trophies to her children, though the weight of a full-grown rat makes her progress across the pasture slow and cumbersome. Mitty usually placed her kill right in front of the kitchen door, sat down and waited for my reaction when I stumbled over a handsome meadowlark or a less appealing and often headless snake. The reaction was forthcoming in either case and it was hardly enthusiastic, so she could not have continued this practice to win my approval. In fact I have never seen any evidence to support the theory that cats try to please humans. Their demeanor would suggest that they are judging rather than being judged. Perhaps that is why some people don't care for cats.

Our pediatrician had a cat who deposited a mouse on his doorstep each morning. After the gift had been acknowledged the cat would eat the mouse. One summer the family was away for a week. Upon their return they found seven mice lined up at the door. When mutual greetings had been exchanged, the cat ate all seven mice, including the six-day-old one!

No cat of ours has found his way hundreds of miles to us when we have moved. For the five years we lived in New York City in the winter and in Vermont in the summer, we had two kittens each summer which were given away when we returned to the city. These cats not only made no effort to find us; they settled down peacefully with their new owners and showed no sign of recognition when we saw them the next year. Perhaps they were too young, the association too short, or our personalities not endearing enough to be worth remembering. A six-year-old friend apparently has the magnetism we lack. Linda went to Europe with her family for a year. Her cat, Whisky (short, of course, for Whiskers), was loaned to a neighbor. After a few weeks the neighbor reluctantly wrote Linda that Whisky not only had not appeared at their door for some time but had not been seen in the neighborhood.

No, Whisky did not stow away on a tramp steamer and spring into Linda's arms from a hedgerow in Devonshire. He was not seen by anyone who recognized him for the rest of the year. The family returned, unpacked their clothes and souvenirs and reclaimed their dog from friends who had boarded the dog in their absence. The next morning, Whisky was sleeping peacefully, curled up next to the dog on the doorstep!

All right! Cats don't, always.

Operation Pine Planting

MY earliest recollection involving trees is of a warped note-book full of pressed leaves, gathered in first grade. I should have seen the handwriting on the blackboard, but being unable to read, my attention was focused on out-collecting the boy in front of me.

From that point on, my communion with trees evolved through skinning the cat, playing Tarzan, building a tree house, and finally carving initials. But never did I envision myself as a tree planter. I took Joyce Kilmer's words to heart and stuck to poetry.

Fortunately my husband's vision has a telescopic if practical sight. He pictured our unused pasture land in Vermont as a nursery in three years, a harvest of fence posts in twelve, and a valuable source of lumber in twenty-five. Before the glaze had melted from his eyes, he teamed up with conservation, the soil bank, and had made a tentative date with the county forester for the following spring.

Deciding to plant eight thousand pine trees and planting them bear about the same relation to each other as buying a ticket to a bull fight and being a matador. For one thing infant trees (four years old in our case), like human babies, don't always arrive on the day you have marked on your calendar. But at least you don't call the obstetrician. The obstetrician, or in this case the nurseryman, phones you, and you suddenly discover that you are about to become the parents of eight thousand baby pines.

I had never picked up eight thousand anything, except

germs, and I couldn't believe that our half-ton pickup truck would even begin to hold that many four-year-old trees. Wrong again. A bale of two thousand pine trees is about the size of a bale of hay, and each bundle of fifty fits as neatly in your hand as the skimpy bunches of daffodils sold in the supermarkets in March.

Let me warn you that directly after you order any variety of evergreen (not before, of course), everyone to whom you recklessly boast of your venture tells you that you have ordered the wrong kind. If you choose white pine, as we did, these arm-chair conservationists will tell you that it takes them too long to grow to marketable size, that blister rust will wipe out any trees which happen to survive the droughts, the floods and the animals which have been waiting around with sharpened teeth. What you should plant, they point out, is Scotch pine. But if you do decide on Scotch pine, they'll tell you that the wood will be of such poor quality that you will be able to see through it. If you order Christmas trees, you'll be told that they will all be stolen. White spruce? Oh, my goodness, no. It has an unpleasant odor. Well, after a while, so has the unsolicited advice. What you plant should be a secret between you and your forester. His advice is not only free but it is sound as well. The novice planter has all the qualms of a new parent. But those tiny trees are tough. They will grow in thin poor soil that doesn't hold enough water to keep grass from withering during the summer months.

We had been warned that young pines should be planted as soon as the frost is out of the ground, which is late April in northern Vermont. Nevertheless we were caught unprepared when we received the phone call announcing that our little pine trees were ready to be picked up. All we needed to do was to round up eight able-bodied planters and six mattocks, and meet the county forester at our farm on Saturday morning.

I knew what eight able-bodied planters were but I didn't know where to find them. I didn't even know what a mattock was, and less about its likely habitat. Somehow we sensed that our farming neighbors would have other things to do besides plant our pine trees all Saturday and Sunday. We were right. Nor does our immediate family consist of eight men strong enough to wield mattocks. Past experience had taught us not to rely on the enthusiasm of our daughters for such projects as devoting a weekend to planting eight thousand pine trees. But, while my husband enlisted the services of three forestry students, I scurried around in search of mattocks.

All our neighbors had shovels and one had a pick, but none had pick-mattocks. Buying them at six dollars apiece would eat into our profits and besides, who wanted to add six mattocks to the confused collection of tools already festooning the garage walls? The son of a local contractor, hearing of our plight through the high school grapevine, offered to loan us his father's mattocks. Happily his father was out of town.

So our little land army, looking about as motley and considerably less dedicated than the Minute Men, headed for the farm. It consisted of my husband and myself, our two daughters, the older daughter's sixteen-year-old boy friend (luring him with the recommended dollar-an-hour high school wage had been a stroke of genius: it turned our daughter's reluctance into burning enthusiasm), and three silent, sleepy and frail-looking forestry students who were paid $1.25 an hour.

We were also laden down with the food I thought we would need for the day on the theory that an army travels on its stomach. The theory was right, but my estimate of the capacity of the stomach must have been based on a hibernating army of pigmies.

The two girls, the boy friend, and I arrived first in the truck. We leapt out and began to flourish the mattocks experimentally. I wobbled the heavy thing up over my shoulder and sank it vigorously into the ground. I tried to pull it out. Nothing happened. I tugged and twisted from all angles and finally dug it out with a shovel. Fortunately, as soon as the forester, my husband and the students arrived, the girls and I were excused from mattock duty.

The plan went like this. The forester roughly indicated rows and started the diggers six feet apart. They were to plunge the mattocks into the ground, the full depth of the blade, pull back and remove the mattock, leaving a wedge-shaped hole, and move on six feet, or two paces, to dig another hole. The girls and I, with bunches of baby pines up to their necks in pails of water (they must *never* dry out even for a minute), followed, placing a small tree in each hole at just the correct depth, firming the soil tight back around the tree by doing a sort of Indian dance around it, stamping the sod back tight around the roots. What a strange Druid ritual this might have appeared to be from a Martian's point of view as we dug, bent and danced in parallel lines up the hillside! One flat meadow was to be planted by a tree-planting machine, hired by the forester. The machine would do three thousand, but that left five thousand for us to get into the ground in two days. Every one of us except the forester thought it couldn't be done. After the first few holes my husband's face was red, and the boys were shedding their heavy jackets. But then that alchemy of second wind, or perhaps it was group dynamics, took over.

The forestry boys wanted to make a good impression on the forester. My husband wanted to prove that he was just as brawny as the college boys. The sixteen-year-old boy had no intention of losing face with his girl in front of the college boys, and the two girls were motivated by the knowledge that they were motivating the boys. And as for me? Oh, I was in there boosting morale all over the place, or could it have been my own ego?

There developed a kind of rhythm and harmony that is hard to describe. The college boys began to look much stronger and more wide awake. The rosy glow on my husband's face revealed more pride than exertion, and behind us, plumes of little pines marched up the hill in neat rows. Jokes began to be tossed back and forth and each one seemed funnier than it really was. A song broke out now and then and echoed back from the granite cliffs. We knocked off for lunch and attacked the platters of baked beans and hot dogs like eight vacuum cleaners. The forester stayed on with us for lunch. In fact he brought his own lunch in a dinner pail neatly packed with thermos bottles of hot soup and coffee. During lunch he told us about trees and other planting operations in our county. Even the girls listened with rapt attention as they stuffed their mouths with hot dogs. We had a stake in the future. We were part of a long-range plan. How long was brought home to me when I remarked that I looked forward to walking among the tall pines, that is if I could ever walk again, I added, stretching my seemingly permanently pleated back.

"Jeepers!" the boy exclaimed. "By the time these pines are tall, you'll be rocking on the porch!"

"Well," I snorted indignantly, "I'll sit in a pine rocker, made from our own lumber."

It wasn't all a spring idyll. There were times when a boy would drive a mattock onto a rock concealed beneath the thin sod and he would wince as the impact shivered up his arms.

Operation Pine Planting

There was also the problem of crossing the brook, swollen by melting snow to the proportions of a young river. There was no way to cross it but to take off our shoes, roll up our jeans and wade in. Have you ever waded knee deep through an ice-rimmed stream in April? We, on the near shore, laughed when the first boy, halfway across the brook, looked back in anguish and moaned that his feet wouldn't move. Our snickers froze along with our toes when the same momentary paralysis gripped each of us in turn. When we stepped out of the brook on the far side into a bank of black-specked shrinking snow, the snow actually felt warm. It wasn't a spectator sport. It was hard steady work for six hours on one day and five the next. But it was the best family fun we had had in a long time. Togetherness was no longer a word. We felt it in every relaxed muscle and it glowed from eight grinning faces. And beyond the momentary satisfaction, there was a further promise. Just as we packed our tools and climbed into the truck, one boy looked around and said, "I'm going to remember just where this place is. Some day I'm going to come back here and show my kids the first pine woods I helped to plant."

Grounded by a Grouse

IF the motifs on Christmas cards are any indication of popular opinion, the average American thinks that a partridge just sits there in his espaliered pear tree watching a tuneful parade of swans, maids and pipers pass in front of his beady little eyes. But if the reason the partridge was chosen for the song was alliteration, as I suspect, they could have used a peacock just as well. Actually a peacock would be more colorful and a lot more likely to be found in an English garden.

Though my knowledge of the mores of partridges is limited, it does include the fact that partridges are not prone to appear at parades or other public performances. In fact Peterson (*A Field Guide to the Birds*) professes that partridges prefer privacy.

So when my husband came hurtling into the house one spring morning complaining that he had been attacked by a grouse, I'm afraid I was something less than sympathetic. I regarded him with what is literarily called a jaundiced eye.

I am not sure that I had ever seen a partridge in its natural habitat at that time, which is as much the bird's fault as mine because you rarely do—see them, that is.

But there was George touching his forehead gingerly and insisting that right in our driveway a ruffed grouse, known as a *pa'tridge* in these parts, had hurled herself at his noggin.

"Impossible," I explained. "What did you do to it?"

"Absolutely nothing! I was minding my own business, raking the old leaves out of the flower bed when this chicken-sized gray-brown bird ran right up to me and slammed into

72

my head. She's probably still out there if you don't believe me."

"Maybe she has a nest nearby. Why don't we feed her some corn and maybe we can get a look at the babies."

So we tiptoed around making noises appropriate for soothing edgy maternal partridges and, being out of pear trees and vague about the preferences of partridges, we scattered corn and apple parings at a discreet distance. The small female ruffed grouse, who looked exactly like the picture above the same name in Peterson's *Field Guide*, regarded us solemnly from her stakeout at the edge of the driveway and ignored our hospitality. She looked so benign and gentle as she leisurely picked her way around under the pine trees that George's complaint was hardly credible.

We have friends who have gone on an African safari armed only with cameras and found themselves overexposed to a rhinoceros who felt rather strongly about his territorial prerogatives. We've also had a spate of acquaintances who have seen the whites of the eyes of a bear or a barracuda. But in recent years the post-prandial and post-brandyal adventure stories seem to lean more towards mugging. In fact one friend was mugged in a parking lot in Washington and when he was released by his attackers and ran down the street looking for help he was mugged again. But whoever heard of being attacked by a grouse? Me, that's who. I not only had to hear about it, I soon joined the ranks of the bad guys in our grouse's estimation.

Later that morning I decided to set out some petunia plants that were languishing in the garage. I wasn't thinking about the grouse and was on my knees digging holes with a trowel, when Thump! something bounced off my nether portions with the impact of a basketball. It was smaller than a basketball and covered with feathers. It was the grouse. I couldn't believe it. I stood up and tried to engage her in casual conversation, assuring her of our friendly feelings but she paced back and forth about a yard away from me making little churring noises.

I was convinced that she either had a nest or a clutch of tiny babies nearby so I carefully explored the entire area but found nothing. She did not play the broken wing ruse to lure me away from any one spot. When I squatted, she squatted. When I walked, she walked. She idly pecked at the ground and I resumed digging. Suddenly she lunged at me again. By this time I was slightly unnerved. I hated to admit that I was afraid of a grouse but who wants to be a backboard for a two-pound ball of fowl? I picked up a rake and flapped it at her. She squnched down the way a hen does when alarmed but didn't budge. Even when I gently pushed at her with the rake she only hopped in place and wouldn't be shooed away. I finally gave up the transplanting and went indoors. A few minutes later she was around at the front of the house where George was unwrapping some rose bushes, circling him determinedly as though seeking out his Achilles' heel.

All day every time either of us stepped outdoors, Mrs. Grouse materialized out of the woods and dogged our footsteps. She couldn't be incubating eggs or she wouldn't stay away from her nest for such long periods of time.

One neighbor stopped to ask if we had noticed the partridge that he had seen several times in our driveway. The mailman honked twice and commented on her presence. John DeBrul, a boy who was hauling wood for us, came running up to the house from halfway down to the brook and breathlessly told me about a big wild bird only a few feet away from him. He was so fascinated that he crawled under the pine tree where she was wandering around and for the next hour they stared at each other in silence. She never attacked John, but his catatonic state didn't pose a threat.

George's tales of being grounded by a grouse were greeted by the raised eyebrows and disbelief of his colleagues. The next Sunday she harassed him until he, too, retreated indoors. She scurried around to the front of the house where she could see him through the picture window from the top of a big rock and dared him to step outside. He took a picture of her which was useful in silencing his friends but did nothing to appease the grouse.

One morning when I was backing the car out of the garage, I heard a thump. I stopped the car, afraid that I had hit her but she had hit me! As I watched she hurled herself at the left rear hubcap again, fluffed out her feathers, and squared off for what might have been her third attack if I hadn't driven out of the yard. She followed the car at a run for a short distance and then started back to the driveway just like a dog who seems to feel that he has driven away a passing car.

We never found a nest or any young though I searched daily and never stepped outside for two weeks without the sensation that I was being followed. I was. She would appear in seconds down at the garden or near the spring no matter how stealthily I tried to sneak out of the house. Frankly she was becoming a nuisance. She had us under virtual house arrest and was wearing my love of nature pretty thin. I am all for conservation but doesn't that include humans too? We returned to Vermont partly because we like country living. Not just any old country: Vermont countryside where the flora and fauna, with whom we can co-exist peacefully, are familiar and benign. The snowshoe hares, deer and birds add to our enjoyment but I have been known to wonder just who is being conserved in June when mosquitoes find me tasty. If I want to share my blood I prefer to do it at the blood bank and not with the black flies.

We are fascinated by the raccoon who on winter nights scoops the peanut butter out of our bird feeder with his delicate little paws, looking over his shoulder at us through his black mask, but I become fiercely competitive with him in August when he and I both want the corn that I have planted and hoed.

So I was beginning to have mixed emotions about this aggressive bird. We had established our territorial prerogative twenty-five years ago when we bought this farm, long before her grandmother was an egg!

We never considered shooting her. George wouldn't and I couldn't because I have never found a way to hold a gun with fingers in both my ears. I wished her no bodily harm but I yearned for the good old days when only an occasional chickadee or red squirrel supervised my outdoor activities.

Then one day no grouse patrol! I basked in a morning spent outdoors unscolded and unscathed. But that evening when we drove down the road we noticed something in the gravel on the shoulder. George backed up and we saw a familiar bundle of gray and brown feathers, limp and lifeless where she must have been struck by a car.

She had stood off two humans and innumerable cars for a month and died on the field of honor defending whatever it was that her instinct told her to protect. Too bad we never found out, but this past holiday season her Christmas card counterparts looked like pretty passive partridges to both of us.

Turkeys

THE only thing dumber than a turkey is a person who thinks it would be fun to raise turkeys. I can't imagine why we did it more than once. Maybe that says something about our intelligence. More likely it was because, after building them an indoor playpen in South Burlington and an outdoor coop in Jericho, it seemed wasteful not to use them. Even as slow learners we had an edge on the turkeys. They seem to be hatched with very little built-in knowledge. A day-old chick or duckling will start pecking at the feed or at anything as soon as his down is dry. Something tells him that his mission in life is to consume as much of his environment as possible before his environment consumes him. But turkey poults will stand near, or more likely in, their feed without grasping the idea that it is edible. You have to shove their beaks in it a few times till the taste sends a slow message to what can be called a brain only if you use the term very loosely.

Turkeys seem to have only one built-in response to any stimulus, panic. They plunge into hysterics when anything approaches, even if it is the hand that has fed them day after day. When they are little they can crowd into a corner and trample each other with few casualties. But when the toms weigh eighteen pounds and the hens twelve, with wing-spreads of six feet, a wave of mob hysteria can send them piling up in one corner of a pen in a huddle which should only happen on a football field. The difference is that football players are protected by padding and helmets and the watchful eye of an official. When a turkey huddle disengages itself the bottom bird may have had his last breath squashed

77

out of him. At least the low man in the football huddle is carried off the field like a hero, with the cheers of thousands ringing in his ears. The turkeys regard their fallen comrade as an uneven bit of the terrain to be stepped on rather than over as they solemnly strut around the pen without the least tweak of conscience or even curiosity.

We kept our twelve turkey poults in the cellar the first six weeks of their lives, not because we wanted to, but because the two parts of the chicken house were bulging with laying hens and day-old chicks. Even if the census hadn't been so high, we had been brainwashed into belief in segregation of poultry. Chickens carry a disease called Black Leg which is Black Death to turkeys. In fact we were warned that we probably couldn't raise both successfully on the same farm. We did, but any sensible farmer's wife wouldn't put up with turkeys in the cellar. George built them a raised cage the size of a four-poster bed, enclosed in wire and with wire mesh where the mattress would normally be. This allowed the droppings to go through the mesh onto the newspaper-covered floor. The farmer's wife was allowed to carry these newspapers out daily and dump them on the asparagus bed for fertilizer. It wasn't my favorite chore, but the alternative, not changing the papers daily, was unthinkable. As it was, by the last week, the whole first floor smelled like the bird house at the zoo. Fortunately it was May and the windows were open to let the fragrance of apple blossoms and lilacs in and, hopefully, the essence of turkey out.

At six weeks the poults were about broiler chicken size and twelve of them could be tucked into a carton to make the seventeen mile journey to Jericho for the summer. If their summer quarters hadn't been outdoors my days of turkey-wifery would have ended right there, but we had a raised, roofed and wire-enclosed coop below the barn just waiting for some sort of feathered folk. It wouldn't work for the laying hens with no nests and it was too small for our large population of adolescent pullets and young roosters, who moved into various parts of the barn that were never intended for poultry. I doubt if anyone else ever converted a horse stall into an apartment for laying hens with the drop-front feed boxes serving as nests, but the hens and Wolfs thought it was great. And the only trouble with the woodshed for the young poultry was that our bedroom abutted on the woodshed. When the cockerels' voices changed and they began to greet the dawn with various dissonant attempts at crowing, all they heralded was their own doom as we carefully selected the noisiest males for Sunday dinner.

Back to the turkeys. They continued to strut and spill their feed and panic at everything from a barn swallow swooping under their overhanging roof, to a jet plane twenty thousand feet overhead. By the end of August, when we had to return with our menagerie to South Burlington, you couldn't have stuffed one, let alone twelve, into a cardboard carton. The only way we could transport them was to tie their wings close to their bodies and their feet together and stuff them individually into grain bags. They didn't enjoy the procedure but neither did we and by the time we had them all trussed up we weren't wasting too much love on each other anyway. Before we learned to tie their wings close, one Tom flapped so violently when we were trying to bag him that he broke his wing. I would have been more sympathetic if he hadn't also almost broken mine. When they were finally back at South Burlington we let them wander loose until Thanksgiving. They gave the farm and barnyard a Currier and Ives look. Having never known freedom, they never heard the call of the wild. Why wander away when food appeared at the kitchen door twice a day?

We had only one major turkey catastrophe and we never knew quite what happened then. Very early one November morning, about five o'clock, I heard a violent commotion outside, a dog barking, the sound of glass breaking and flapping and squawking. George was out of town. I dashed into Debbie's room to look out her window, where the noise seemed to be coming from. Below her window there was a cold frame where small tomato plants got a head start in spring so that they could be transplanted to the garden as soon as all danger of frost was past. The cold frame was smashed, a turkey disappearing around the corner of the house and an unfamiliar dog was dragging another protesting turkey across the meadow. By the time I got into my jeans and shirt, the dog had vanished, his turkey victim lay dying in the field, two other turkeys were gobbling hysterically and the cold frame was not only a shambles with the plants strewn and broken, but one of our kittens was dead in the cold frame. No sign of being strangled or bitten. I could only guess that the dog and the turkey thrashed around on the cold frame and our curious little kitten got caught in the path of destruction. The girls and I had a dreary breakfast with noticeable loss of appetite. As a matter of fact I think it was the last year we raised turkeys. But still, like having a baby, it was something I wouldn't want to do again now, but neither would I have missed the drama.

And somehow at Thanksgiving, in our one-hundred-and-fifty-year-old farmhouse, when we sat down to celebrate an early American tradition, it seemed fitting that almost everything on the table had been grown by us on our farm, the sausage in the stuffing, the apples and pumpkin in the pies, the potatoes, onions, parsley and squash, and especially the great golden-brown bird, for once in his stupid life smelling delicious, looking handsome, mourned by none but the focus of all admiring eyes.

Pig in a Bucket

I SHOULD no longer be surprised that our pleasure in raising pigs is not an emotion widely shared. In any group there are those who champion tropical fish, Labrador retrievers, or tuberous begonias, but not pigs. This wouldn't surprise me in Manhattan, or even in Westchester. But in northern Vermont even those who live in the country but earn their living in the nearby city suffer sporadic attachments to saddle horses, a small flock of sheep or some bantam chickens. This attachment, however, does not seem to extend to pigs, even among our neighbors, most of whom are dairy farmers.

When a recent guest, a psychiatrist, explained in great detail that his success in trout fishing was based on his ability to think like a trout, I exclaimed happily, "Of course! The same thing is true in catching pigs."

The ensuing silence and tolerant glances in my husband's direction indicated that, in the minds of the other guests, the psychiatrist's time in our home would be better spent professionally than socially.

On the way to thinking like a trout, the psychiatrist used many years and half the equipment in L. L. Bean's catalogue. The same thing has been achieved by intuitive country boys with garden worms and a willow wand.

Twice a year the psychiatrist escapes from the demands of his work and renews his strength with a fishing vacation. Twice a year we cannot escape from the fact that our two pigs are large enough to be butchered, and that we must renew the diminishing stock of pork in the freezer. We share

81

two things in common with the psychiatrist. Both he and we can eat the products of our efforts, and both he and we backed into our respective skills through learning how NOT to catch our quarry.

There are all sorts of books on trout fishing, some with yellow sou'wester waterproof covers, so that you may go right on reading when you step into a deep hole and begin feeling like a trout. I have never seen a book on catching and loading pigs into a half-ton truck. It probably wouldn't be a fast moving item in most book stores.

We keep two pigs all the time for a variety of reasons. We have a large barn at a good distance from the house. They save us money in food bills. They require a minimum of care, and most important but least understood, we like pigs.

However, twice a year they must be loaded into the truck and taken to the slaughterhouse. A seven-month-old pig weighs about two hundred and fifty pounds, which is distributed in such a streamlined fashion that there is nothing to hang on to. Even if you could put a halter on a pig, it cannot be pulled. The harder you pull, the harder the pig pulls the other way, and the pig has the edge on most of us in weight. Shoving won't work either, even if you have another pig fancier pulling on the front end. The pig, screeching in blood-curdling tones, whether you are holding a leg or an ear, will thrash and twist out of your grasp.

The first time we were faced with this problem was ten years and forty-six pigs ago. The memory of that morning is still too painful to describe objectively. We tried to fasten ropes around the pigs, but they slithered loose. We chased them through the garden and fields. Finally, by luck rather than skill, we cornered the two pigs in the barn where they were confined, though far from being loaded in the back of the Jeep station wagon. Shaken and bruised from head to foot, George leaned against the barn door and threatened to shoot the pigs. Only the fact that he was too exhausted to move postponed their doom. Hours later, we finally dragged the shrieking, floundering pigs up a wooden ramp into the wagon and set off on a limp journey to town.

In true Vermont fashion, none of our neighbors offered unsolicited advice to George. But when I described our struggle to one friend, he told me that all you had to do was put a bucket over a pig's head and back it to whatever destination you had in mind. When he added that it helped if someone else grabbed the tail and steered the pig, I suspected that my city-bred leg was being pulled once more, and dismissed his words from my mind.

It was not until the next summer that I remembered his suggestion and offered it tentatively to George. Softened by the memory of bruises and a sprained knee, my husband agreed to let me try. I put a little grain in the bottom of a pail and climbed into the pen with the pigs. While George knocked off the boards on one side, I enticed the pig to try a bite. The moment her head was in the bucket, George grabbed her tail, while I pushed from the bucket end, and all three of us sailed out of the pig pen, up through the barnyard and were inside the Jeep in three minutes!

It could't be true. It was too easy; just luck. So with some doubts, the next season we once again started to load pigs.

This time it was early morning, and George and I were going to load the pigs before he went to his office. We had only half an hour. When neither pig showed any interest in the pail, George lunged at them and all was lost. He and the two pigs chased each other around making angry noises. We gave up and went in for breakfast.

After breakfast, with George at work and the children at school, I began to wonder. The Jeep was still parked halfway in the barn door. The ramp was in place on the tailgate. Could I . . . ? Would it be possible to load those two pigs by myself? If I got one in the station wagon, could I keep it there while I loaded the other? With pounding heart, I planned my strategy. First I put an appetizing mound of lettuce leaves in the back of the Jeep. Then I mixed some grain and water in the pail. Singing Brahms's Lullaby with words improvised for pig loading, I held the pail in the pigpen and tried to act disinterested. Immediately one pig thrust her snout in the pail. I jammed it farther onto her head and backed her out of the pen. The ramp was narrow, and without George's guiding hand on the curly rudder, she backed off the side on to the barn floor. But I stayed with her, keeping the pail over her head and shoving with all my strength. The air was limited in the pail. She was gasping. So was I. The thought that she was weakening gave me second wind and we plunged up the ramp into the Jeep. She immediately became engrossed in the lettuce, as I had hoped, and I crawled out to find the other pig.

He was grunting curiously at the tailgate. I slammed the pail over his head and backed him in a wide arc so that his rear end would come around to the wooden ramp. There's a lot of strength in a pig. I was losing mine rapidly along with the skin from several knuckles. My arms were quivering from exertion. Halfway up the ramp he began to fold his hind legs under him and sit down.

"Please . . . ," I gasped. "Please get in there!"

I shut my eyes and strained till little lights danced before my eyes. Miraculously, the pig backed up the ramp and into the Jeep. With shaking hands I closed the tailgate and leaned against it, panting. I was dripping wet. I was also streaked with a gruel of grain and water. I staggered into the front seat and slowly drove off with my shifting, grunting cargo.

Pig in a Bucket

It wasn't necessary to go past George's office to get to the slaughterhouse; in fact it was quite a bit out of the way. But there are times when the shortest distance is beside the point. The driveway at the Medical College went right under the windows of George's office. I pulled up beneath the windows and serenaded him with the horn. The pigs added their hoarse baritones. No response, so I leaned on the horn with more than necessary fervor. I had hoped to see George, but in a moment four heads appeared at the windows. A family affair was one thing, but I was hardly dressed for an executive committee meeting. Four jaws dropped. Four noses were grasped between thumb and forefinger, and four mouths burst into laughter.

There are a few moments in life which are too tightly packed with emotion to allow space for words. The laughter was applause, and I was giddy with pride.

Life Up-Country  **IV**

Goldfish Bowls Are for Fish

ONE of the advantages of country living is that I am rarely observed doing the bizarre things that come quite naturally to me. What I do in the garden or at the brook is mercifully between me and a few monarch butterflies. Of course our house is near enough to the road so that when I return from the garden dressed in George's 1930 trench coat and the Army and Navy store net headgear that keeps me and the black flies at a respectful distance from each other, the occasional car that passes at that moment has been known to waver slightly as the driver tries to figure out whether I'm robbing a beehive or concealing disfiguring scars I got when someone threw acid in my face. The passing motorist may also wonder why we have an old rusty sap pan under the rainspout and a row of buckets on the sagging front doorstep. It has nothing to do with maple. The fact is our well is nearly dry and we collect rainwater in the pan, dip it out with the buckets and pour it into the back of the toilet so that we can continue to enjoy indoor plumbing in spite of the drought.

No one sees us attach a three-foot length of galvanized leader to the end of the pipe at our spring halfway down the hillside and set a pail under it. That's for drinking water. And the ancient washing machine which sits outdoors on a wooden platform that George built for it is at the back of the house, not from modesty but simply because that's where the clothesline is. We run a hose from the kitchen sink out through the bathroom window into the washing machine. That's to fill it. To drain it we just pull the plug and let gravity carry the water down the hillside. I'm glad no one can see how often I get a washcloth caught in the wringer. That's partly because the wringer is temperamental and partly because there is so much to divert my attention, a goldfinch swaying on a milkweed blossom or a wasp hovering above my left ear.

We have an outdoor shower which actually is in plain sight from the road and yet the occupant is invisible because of a camouflaged enclosure George built. The slats that enclose it on two sides are slanted so that the washee can see out but the passerby only sees what looks like a white board enclosure. It's a bit unnerving the first time you lather up fifteen feet from the road but after the first few frosts in late September, a hot shower is a big improvement over an icy bath in the brook. That shower would have caused eyebrows to arch a bit in Weston, Massachusetts, and even higher in Mission Hills, Kansas, two handsome suburbs we lived in before we returned to Vermont.

Now that we are going to be year-round summer folk we are installing a few more creature comforts. In fact we are installing a whole new house from sheer necessity. The old one, built in 1820, remains upright only from habit. The cellar stones are caving in, the sills are rotten and we don't dare poke the beams anymore. The last poke sent up a cloud of dust like a puff ball and the next poke might be the straw that broke the cantilever's back.

But even in our new house I imagine we will cling to patterns which seem normal only to us. Spring water is kept in a row of half-gallon whisky bottles which adorn one end of the kitchen counter. Eight half-gallon whisky bottles looks like quite a party and might get us referred to the local chapter of the W.C.T.U. if they saw me filling the coffee pot and pouring the water over the potatoes from them.

Goldfish Bowls Are for Fish

If we don't feel like wading through the tall dewy grass to the clothesline we can get our bathing suits and towels by hanging out the living room window and reeling them in just the way the housewives do in the tenements of New York.

This year I've been very glad that some of my gardening habits have not been widely observed. We have had so many uninvited raccoons, deer, rabbits and woodchucks to dinner that, in an effort to have some vegetables left for the Wolfs, I now cover the beans and peas each night with big sheets of plastic. An old shower curtain and bed sheets are tied around the pole beans and cabbages and broccoli wear ancient waste baskets and pails that have been demoted from water duty because they have sprung leaks.

Probably the time I was the most grateful for the dense cover of woods around our brook was years ago when the children were small. We often picnicked at the pool and had built a makeshift stone fireplace there. We also bathed in the brook and one sunny day we got the idea that we could do the laundry down there. This was before we even had our tolerant old wringer machine and doing the laundry involved a trip to town to the laundromat. So we built a fire, filled an old copper boiler with water, heated it on the stone fireplace, added soap and the clothes and swished them around with sticks. Then we poled them out and heaved them into the pool where the children sloshed them up and down to rinse them and George and I wrung them out. When the clothes were done we lifted the boiler off onto the grass and the two little girls took turns in the boiler, small blond heads just poking over the rim. It was all so warm and sudsy and inviting that when they climbed out and dashed for the brook, I pulled off the last items of the minimal summer outfit I had been wearing, climbed into the boiler with my rags and swished around washing them and me simultaneously. This seemed quite logical to me at the time but this summer, twenty-four years later, when I read in the local paper that a young man in Vermont had received a jail sentence for swimming in the nude I was incensed. So were a lot of other people. It finally reached *Time* magazine, where Vermont state's attorney Patrick Leahy was quoted as saying, "On private land out of view of the public, the state has no legitimate interest. In secluded areas sometimes publicly used, if no member of the public present is offended, no disorderly conduct has taken place."

I'm glad that skinny-dipping for small boys in the old swimming hole has not been outlawed. Isn't it almost one of the American freedoms? And I'm glad that what a young mama chooses to wear or not to wear in her own forest pool won't come to the attention of the Supreme Court. Actually I've reached the age when I know that clothes are a girl's best friend. But the *right* to splash privately as unencumbered as Botticelli's Venus, or trussed up in an Annette Kellerman bathing dress, high laced canvas swimming shoes and carrying a parasol, I stoutly defend. Isn't that part of what living in the country is all about?

Of Pumps and Dumps

A FRIEND of ours commented one day that it was easy to distinguish a city-bred child from a country-bred child. Not by their knowledge of nature or Broadway. It was simply that a country child felt guilty when he flushed a toilet and a city child felt guilty when he didn't.

Our younger daughter, at the age of ten, announced that the prime requisite for her husband would be his solemn promise to live somewhere where they would be supplied with city water. Never mind the richer or poorer lines. First things first.

But I wonder if our country-reared children haven't picked up a certain responsibility for their environment which must be contrived for those in the city if they are to acquire it at all. Every summer when we have a good many guests, this is apparent. We race about turning off faucets that are left running, picking out smoldering cigarette butts that are tossed in a wastebasket, and separating cans and broken glass from the burnable trash, while our guests, adult and child alike, stare at us in bewilderment and condescension.

"You certainly do make life complicated," one guest remarked when I scooped out the food scraps that she had scraped into the sink.

We don't have a Dispos-All. We don't need one even if our septic tank would tolerate it. We use all our garbage. It doesn't seem complicated to us and it is very gratifying. The cats get the meat and egg scraps. Chickens will eat everything but onion skins, potato peelings, coffee grounds and bones, and these go on the compost heap. The compost heap

93

goes on the garden and the garden vegetables go into us, completing a nice round sensible cycle. We like it that way.

Not all people who live in the country have cats and chickens, and this presents certain garbage problems. Of course you can bury your garbage and enrich the soil, but have you ever tried to do much digging in soil where the frost level is about two feet deep? And garbage that is shallowly buried has a way of being dragged onto the front lawn by the neighbors' dogs. Country dogs are no better at returning old bones to the compost heap than city dogs. In fact they seem to feel responsible for a wide distribution of such treasures.

We have one neighbor, another doctor, who used to take his garbage in neat wrapped parcels to the hospital incinerator. When his wife was away one summer, the bundles accumulated, and because he was familiar with the effect of heat on garbage, our friend popped the wrapped garbage packages into the freezer for temporary storage. But domesticity was not his speciality; having disposed of them, he promptly forgot them.

Sometime later, after his wife had returned, she was trying to think up a new casserole and decided to see what she had in the freezer. She has never quite recovered from the shock of opening five packages of frozen coffee grounds, egg shells and chicken bones. Their dinner that night came from a can, with a clear factual label of contents on the outside.

Of course a family accumulates more trash than just garbage. In fact when I think of how much burnable trash I have lugged out to the backyard incinerator daily and how many boxes of bottles, cans, odd sneakers and flash bulbs we have taken to the dump, I marvel that there is anything left in the house at all. I wondered how this could be until I thought about the shampoo bottle. It's all the advertising man's fault! First, the shampoo is put in an elongated hourglass-shaped container that has at least an inch of solid glass at the base which creates the illusion that the consumer is getting a huge bottle of shampoo for sixty-nine cents. He gets a huge bottle but very little shampoo. Then the bottle is placed in a box much larger than the bottle and the box is put in a paper bag. Clearly the advertising man lives in a city apartment where he can casually drop bottle, bag and box down the incinerator chute at the end of the hall. He doesn't know that my trips to the backyard incinerator to burn the boxes and bags, and to the dump with his heavy, shapely, empty bottles are making me look with favor on a cake of soap.

I like almost all aspects of country living except listening to hear whether or not the pump is in good voice. But there are a few jobs that I regard with mixed feelings. I like to have gone to the dump but I don't like to go there. I am very pleased with myself when the back hall is no longer crammed with cartons of cans, bottles, and bent coat hangers, but the dump itself disturbs me. I can understand the decomposition of organic matter into nice black compost, but I can't believe that the mountains of cans, bottles, old tires, and battered stoves will really become part of Mother Earth even after the bulldozer has shoved tons of sand over them. I dread the day when our great-grandchildren will find that everywhere they dig, for a house foundation, a swimming pool or a mud pie, they will resurrect non-returnable beer bottles and the like as their heritage of our lives.

And the so-called caretakers of the dump disturb me. They are frequently as worn out in appearance as the used up fragments of living from which they eke a living. We have one who immediately pokes through our junk searching for bits of aluminum which he sells, or for personal treasures which he hoards. As our children have grown older, the picking among the discarded broken toys has become very slim, but he was delighted last spring when he found a little case of tiny Coca Cola bottles that the girls had once had in their doll house. He squatted down on the litter-strewn dirt and slipped them in and out of their case murmuring, "Oh, I love them teeny tiny sody bottles."

You can't be cross with a man like that, but I feel uneasy somehow, especially since he is about six feet tall and as wide as Santa Claus.

I can't help thinking how happy he might have been with Scarededy, our cat who lived up to his name. Scarededy's entrance into our life was unique in our experience with cats. When he was about three weeks old, he was found in the back of a truck used to collect rubbish from a few houses in our neighborhood. When he was discovered, the anxious driver of the truck presented him at once to neighbors of ours who are unfortunately allergic to cats. So, of course, he was soon added to our cat family which at that time numbered six or seven. Although Scarededy was treated just like any of our other cats, adored and ignored to a various extent, he has never in his three years with us recovered from the unknown trauma of his first three weeks. I wonder if he had been undiscovered until the rubbish truck was unloaded at the dump, and had been scooped up in the great paws of the dump caretaker, what this meeting might have meant to them both. Oh, well, if the kitten had been run over by one of the many cars and trucks backing and turning at the dump, it would have broken the big man's heart. He doesn't miss the little kitten he never knew and he does have the "sody" bottles to play with.

Lady in the Dark

"YOU wanted a farm in Vermont," I told myself as the lightning and thunder ripped the leaden skies simultaneously over our little white farmhouse in Jericho Center. I held my breath, knowing that at any minute our mysteriously-grounded phone would react to a nearby bolt of lightning with a firecracker retort and a blue flash of light in the living room.

Yes, I had wanted the farm in Vermont, but the first summer I had been slightly dismayed at the thought of staying there alone except on weekends, when George flew up from New York. But the doctor's wife learns early that the pleasure of his company is a sometime thing. Of course I wasn't entirely alone. Our older daughter, Patty, was five that first summer. Debbie was two-and-a-half. There were two kittens, two pigs, twelve chickens and a goat in the barn, none of them bearing much resemblance to a knight in shining armor, or even a smartly breeched state trooper. They made me brave though, maybe not above and beyond the call of duty but adequate thereunto. When a child is afraid, there isn't any alternative for the adult except courage. The picture of myself cowering behind a kitten or a wide-eyed two-year-old never has had much appeal.

I must admit that there were at least three times when the Unknown woke me in the difficult hours of the night and gave me pause. Pause, nothing! It scared the wits out of me.

My first nocturnal moment of rather-not-facing the truth occurred one moonless night the first summer we were in

Life Up-Country

Jericho. I woke with the disquieting sense of impending doom with which I have since grown familiar. What had wakened me I didn't know. I sat up in bed, open-mouthed to hear better.

Step, step, step, scrunch. I reached for my bathrobe with dampening hands. Step, step, scrunch. Someone was walking heavily and slowly around the back of the house. I felt my way down the narrow, steep stairs and crept quietly into the bathroom. The footsteps were just outside. It was pitch dark. I pressed my face against the window and leaped back.

Two enormous eyes were a few inches from my face. A large, rough tongue curled out around two wide nostrils. Daisy, Wayne Nealy's Jersey cow, and I were regarding each other in mutual shock. She snorted and hightailed off to more private pastures, and I wobbled back to bed, snickering to myself in relief.

The next summer I awoke one night thinking that one of the girls was having a bad dream and crying. I crept to Debbie's crib but the only sound was a soft thumb-sucking. Patty was sound asleep across the room. But the crying sound came again, outside. I listened and it came again, loud moaning sounds which stopped and then were repeated at intervals. Something was hurt in our barn! When Hamlet said, "Conscience doth make cowards of us all," he forgot to add that after it makes you feel like a coward, it keeps comparing your liver to a lily. I enjoyed one more cowardly moment of hiding my head under the pillow but the crying came through both the pillow and the fingers in my ears.

"Who's in charge here?" I asked myself sternly.

"You wanted a farm in Vermont," I reminded myself as I put on my sneakers.

"Nobody made you stay here alone," I taunted me as I groped for a flashlight and lumped into my bathrobe. "Something is in trouble in the barn and you and your chicken heart, which is resounding in your ears, have got to do something about it."

So down the stairs I went, out the front door and across the dewy lawn. I *could* have gone through the back hall and the shed, past the sleeping chickens, but somehow the space of the great outdoors seemed preferable to the cobwebs and dark shadows of the woodshed. The crying became louder. It seemed to come from the barn floor. The flashlight slipped in my wet hand and I held my breath as I turned the beam of light on the open space between the two lofts.

There lay Michael, our goat, completely hamstrung, hobbled and hog-tied in his own rope. With every moan and struggle he pulled the rope tighter around his slender legs. It wasn't easy to loosen him. He had pulled the rope so tight that the knots seemed welded together, and he didn't help much with his thrashing and jerking. But the sight of that silly white goat trussed up like a Thanksgiving turkey— instead of the wounded gunman or demented hermit, or a woman in childbirth, or, well, try it on *your* imagination in the middle of the night—was such a relief that I hugged his furry neck and looked with love into those impassive eyes for the first time since he'd lost his kiddish charm.

It was a ridiculous picture, a frowsy woman in a long plaid bathrobe hugging a goat on a barn floor in the middle of the night. But it was so peaceful and sweet-smelling in the barn. The lofts were filled with new-mown hay, the hens shuffled on their roost and settled for another hour's sleep and Michael sighed and stretched his legs in comfort.

When the girls grew big enough to sleep through the night, so did I. Snow could hiss against the windows, our old house could creak and settle in the cold, rain could drum on the roof and I slept on. But one summer weekend after we had moved to Boston, I went up to Jericho with several of Debbie's friends. There were four sixteen-year-old girls and after they had rolled up their hair and licked the last pizza crumbs at about one o'clock, I thought the worst was over.

The girls were quiet but it was a windy night. Branches of the big elm were dancing and waving wildly, and I finally shut the window because the plastic curtains kept flapping so noisily. As I crawled back in bed, I heard a thump, thump on the front door. I had heard no car in the drive. I had seen no lights. I waited, breathing open-mouthed again. Thump, thump. It was the front door all right, I decided, but it didn't sound like the usual rap, rap, rap of a knock. (No one in the country has a doorbell.) There must be someone at the door. I was sleeping (I use the word loosely) in the downstairs bedroom. The four girls were upstairs. True, I had plenty of company, but judging by Janet's screams during a thunderstorm and the concerted shrieks at the sight of a mouse, I had no desire to add their hysteria to my own qualms.

So once again I slid out of bed to face the Unknown. Thump, thump came the heavy sound on the door. I peered cautiously out the side window, and came face to face with my intruder. One of the porch screens, warped over the winter, had blown in. Lifted spasmodically by the wind, it was knocking against the door. I righted it, shut the door and once again, wiser and not the least sad, went back to bed.

The country, and particularly the Vermont countryside, is full of mysteries—the flaming maples in the fall, the flow of their sap in the spring, the squeak of snow under your boots in the sub-zero weather, the way a cow will go to the same stall every afternoon to be milked. We can't explain these things but they fill us with wonder and delight. The mysteries are not frightening, and my few frightened moments in Vermont were not mysteries. A cow, a goat and a screen. They were jokes of nature played by a poker-faced, rock-ribbed countryside on the soft city dweller to test his mettle.

The Law and I

I DON'T make a habit of taking the law into my own hands. I've only done it once. But since this venture has raised more eyebrows than questions, and stopped conversation rather than stimulated it, I have been led to believe that I am something of a deviant.

As a matter of fact I have no compulsion to exceed the speed limit, embezzle two million dollars, or keep a dog without a license. I don't even want to keep a dog anymore, but that's neither here nor there and I'm glad it's not here. I gave up stealing after my first try at the age of eleven, when I discovered that I really had no use for the green celluloid frog I had purloined from the five and ten. I took it back, not because I felt my act had been illegal, but simply because I didn't want it after all. It did occur to me that the salesgirl might not be wise enough to appreciate my point of view, so I merely slipped it back on the counter as surreptitiously as I had removed it. Lightning did not strike, and I rode my bike home basking in the assurance that justice and I were on friendly terms.

The law and I lived happily, if not intimately, ever after, until recently, when presumably I was beyond filching toys.

There is nothing unusual about the traffic in our nearby city. There is just too much of it. The city fathers, tired of complaints, decided to change several two-way arteries into one-way streets. This meant that on one side of the street the parking meters would be at the rear of the parking spaces instead of the front. During the first days of this transition period, I parked the car, dropped my nickel in the meter at

102

the front as usual, went about my business and came back, five minutes later, to find a ticket on the windshield.

I was incensed. In my mind I had broken no law. There was no sign to indicate the change and I had paid above and beyond the call of duty. So, taking the law into my own hands literally, I tore up the ticket and gave it no further thought. But the law does not like to be ignored. You can go along with it, or fight it, or break it, but you must never whistle and walk away from it.

Several nights later we were entertaining a group of dignitaries from various universities, when there was a loud, imperious pounding on the door. My husband opened the door and faced a policeman, armed to the teeth and glaring at him belligerently.

"Does Margaret Wolf live here? I have a summons for her to appear in Municipal Court Saturday morning at ten."

Now Margaret is a perfectly good name. If my parents had happened to name me Margaret I would answer to it happily. But my name is Marguerite. A mere trifle, but can you imagine the reaction if you referred to the former First Lady as Lady Bug Johnson? The man in blue was off to a poor start.

My husband turned to the hushed group, including rosy-visaged me, and with forced gaiety asked if I cared to comment. Our children, theoretically in bed, catapulted down the stairs and assuming that the long arm of the law was about to remove their sandwich maker and knot untier, moaned that Mommy was going to jail.

Bewildered, but with a growing suspicion that the parking business might be involved, I volunteered that I knew of nothing except a silly old parking ticket which I had torn up.

"You tore up a parking ticket?"

All faces turned towards me with expressions of horror and admiration, but the policeman looked as though I had told him to stop playing cops and robbers and go wash his hands before supper.

I still, however, could not seem to fit into the hair shirt. On Saturday morning I marched into the dreary courtroom as unrepentant as a court reporter.

It was great fun to watch the judge, the sullen teenage leather jackets, and cooled-off drunks with whom I shared the dubious comfort of a hard bench. I was enjoying the scene immensely, when my name was called and the judge rapped out, "Guilty or not Guilty?"

"I don't know," I countered brilliantly.

The judge leaned back wearily, shoved up his glasses and patiently lowered his voice to the pitch reserved for frightened children or confused senior citizens.

"Perhaps you'd like to explain?"

"I'd love to!" I exclaimed, and told him how I had parked the car well within the white lines, pushed in my nickel, and gone to exchange Debbie's blue jeans for a larger size.

"Besides," I added, "there was no sign at either end of the street referring to the meters. I looked, when I found the ticket. And so I tore up the ticket and deposited the remains in the waste paper container on the corner."

The judge bit his lip and smiled at the pile of papers in front of him. He turned to my guardian policeman and asked if it was true that there were no notices indicating the change in paying position between fore and aft. The policeman looked uncomfortable, conferred with a colleague and they agreed there were none.

"Case dismissed," the judge announced and I sailed out of the courtroom under the envious gaze of my fellow culprits.

I did not feel elated, nor did I think that I had put one over on the law. I simply felt that justice was elastic, as it should be. I was also glad not to have to pay the $7.20 and costs which would have been the fee had I been pronounced guilty. After all, it was only two days before Christmas. But I did expect my husband to be roughly seven times as pleased as he is dejected when I get, and pay, a dollar parking fine.

The reasoning of the male mind proceeds in a more orderly fashion than that of the female, says the male. He felt that it was unfair for me to get off free. I was guilty of ignoring the ticket whether or not I was guilty of overtime parking.

The pre-Christmas bustle left no time for such dreary splitting of hairs. Towards nightfall we took the children to the school where the P.T.A. was selling Christmas trees. We chose one and were about to pay for it when the salesman emerged in the person of the same policeman who had summoned me to court.

"You!" he gasped, looking as though I were Marley's ghost.

"Yes," my husband agreed wearily. "It looks as though you'll get a chance to see our money after all. How much do we owe you?"

"Well, let's see," the cop grinned. "One dollar for the ticket, $7.20 for the court summons and $1.50 for the tree. It should be $9.70 but I'm only here as a parent volunteer selling Christmas trees, so let's call it $1.50 and Merry Christmas!"

Country Church Mouse

THE Jericho Center church mouse may be as poor as tradition would have him, but he certainly is rich in entertainment. Do funny things happen more often in village churches or does it just seem that way because of the heroic effort to stifle the snicker or snort that would be more anonymous in a larger congregation?

When I was a child my family and almost every one of our neighbors in Montclair, New Jersey, went to church every Sunday. I not only went to church but to Sunday School before church, Junior Choir practice on Friday afternoons and Young Peoples' every Sunday evening. It never occurred to me to protest but I did hunger for any scrap of levity in the behavior or appearance of the congregation or in the hymns and anthems which unfortunately concerned themselves largely with cherubim, seraphim and the washing of spiritual laundry in the blood of the Lamb. It helped to sing "Thy consecrated cross-eyed bear" and because Shirley Davis was a friend, I insisted that "Shirley, goodness and mercy" would follow me all the days of my life, but I can't remember any really funny episodes.

By the time we bought the farm in Jericho Center I was thirty-five years old and presumably could partake of divine services or leave them alone. The First Congregational Church of Jericho was the center of the village, geographically as well as socially and spiritually. In my effort to camouflage the stigma of being "from away," I decided to go to church and of course five-year-old Patty and two-and-a-half-year-old Debbie wanted to come with me. Neither had been to a church service before. On the way I had coached them briefly about being quiet and the proper procedure when the collection would be taken. Each was provided with a nickel for this event, clutched firmly in a small damp fist. We sat towards the back in case a hasty exit became mutually desirable and I put Debbie on the aisle so that she could see without trying to stand on the pew.

Patty, delighted with the furtive smiles from the congregation, smiled back happily and settled down to the serious business of showing off as a perfect little lady. Debbie, also sensing that she was the cynosure of all roving eyes, found it heady enough to pursue further. Before I could grab the bow of her sash she slipped off the pew and out into the aisle. The Reverend Lillian Gregory continued with her sermon and I froze hoping that Debbie would scuttle back at any moment. But, encouraged by the smiles she was provoking, Debbie marched towards the pulpit, smiling and waving to right and left, turned around at the altar, raised her short dress over her head and in her high clear voice invited the assembled multitude to "see my fat tummy." Miss Gregory never faltered and Debbie, having reached the end of her limited repertoire, walked back up the aisle, climbed up on the seat beside me and sighed with satisfaction.

I anchored her firmly with my right arm and whispered that she must stay in her seat so that she could put her nickel in the collection plate. She watched Stanley Bicknell and Ralph Nealy make their way slowly up the aisle and eagerly lifted her nickel up over the edge and dropped it in. But as they moved along her expression turned from eager anticipation to anguish.

"Mommy," she wailed, "I paid Stanley my nickel and he never gave me any of his pie."

This past summer a conference of reading teachers was

being held at the University of Vermont and they decided, as part of their program, to have a country church supper followed by a "light" talk in the First Church in Jericho. I was to be the speaker, and a little uneasy about speaking from a pulpit, I decided to speak from the floor. Debbie, now twenty-five years old and a teacher herself, thought it would be fun to come to hear me. It was the first time that she and I had been back in that church together and as I stood in front of that altar the memory of her aplomb while standing on that same spot was very tranquilizing.

I didn't pull my dress up over my head, deciding wisely that neither the audience nor I would find an exhibition of my fat tummy entertaining, but they laughed at my stories and I found myself warming to their response as Debbie had years before.

We turned up *en famille* at that church again this summer, all except Patty who was in Finland, but George was with us this time, momentarily expecting the roof to fall on his head from the shock of his presence within those consecrated walls. The occasion was Jackie Cross's wedding to Ed Engstrom. The Cross family had moved recently to Jericho Center from Montreal and although Jackie lived in Calgary she thought a country wedding would be appropriate. There was a polished up horse and buggy waiting to drive the bride and groom around the village green in style. The ceremony was in progress inside the church when the two bagpipers, imported from Canada, gay in their Black Watch tartans, arrived to pipe the wedding party out of the church. The Vermont horse took one look at the pipes, kilts and sporrans, erupted from his harness and bolted across the fields before they had played a note. Only seconds later when the bridal party emerged from the church, the best man and the ushers rose to the occasion, picked up the shafts of the buggy and pulled the beaming bride and groom around the green.

Just at that moment the New Hampshire National Guard, scheduled to have a rendezvous with the Vermont National Guard at the nearby artillery range, roared through the village, with lorries full of soldiers, caissons and howitzers. We all stood on the church steps staring dumbly until Alec Mactavish, towering above us, glanced from the procession of howitzers to the mesmerized wedding guests and announced in a voice that carried clearly above the clattering of the military, "I've heard of shotgun weddings but this is ridiculous!"

Our Snow-Covered Welcome Mat

❦❦

SKIING and I go hand in glove. A clammy hand in a frozen glove. Like gray hair, it looked enormously attractive until I was stuck with it. Nothing in my childhood prepared me for life at the foot of Mt. Mansfield. Of course I had shuffled around on some hand-me-down hickories in my corduroy knickers and black canvas Arctics. That was when bindings were strips of flannel worn around a baby's stomach. But skiing wasn't a prestige sport in Montclair in the Twenties. It was another way of having fun in the snow along with belly-flopping on Flexible Flyers and making snowmen with lumps of coal for eyes. Slalom and status had nothing to do with each other. I doubt if our parents had ever heard of either, except where status was followed by quo.

Even when I was in college in the Thirties, and in New England too, serious skiing was only for those hardy girls, the same ones who charged around the hockey field while the rest of us, grotesque in black leotards, expressed our rampant emotions through The Medium of the Dance.

Of course we had ski suits, from Bamberger's or Filene's, thick woolen ones with baggy pants and knitted cuffs at the ankle. They came without skis, though, and so did we. The public excuse was that the ski suits were to be worn to classes during very cold weather, but privately we hoped to be invited to the Dartmouth Winter Carnival where a ski suit was *de rigueur* even if the wearer thought that Christina was a girl's name.

110

Our Snow-Covered Welcome Mat

I understand that skiing boomed during the Forties, but the only booms involving most of us were those of guns and babies. Stowe and Sun Valley were as remote from our world of furloughs and feedings as Acapulco and Bali Ha'i. We dreamed of them, but the immediate challenge was to drag through the next invasion or the 2:00 A.M. feeding.

Then came the Fifties, scattering us across the country into ranch houses and split-levels or kindly, in our case, into a very old farmhouse.

There skiing, or the Abominable Snow Mania, replaced the wolf at the door—no pun intended. Long-forgotten buddies from college, overseas units, or Christmas card acquaintances arrived in Volkswagens, Thunderbirds and jalopies prickly with skis. The old familiar scents of diapers and croup kettles were supplanted by hot wax and wet wool.

I know that Maine lobstermen rarely know how to swim and don't intend to learn. This may be impractical, but it is not regarded as immoral. During the fifteen years we lived in Manhattan, we avoided the Empire State Building, the Statue of Liberty and Grant's Tomb without losing face.

"Of course you ski," murmur our metropolitan friends, swiveling the onions clockwise in their Gibsons. It is stated as a fact, but I am mulish enough to take it as a question.

"No, I don't," I say.

The effect is the same as if I had become hysterical and disclosed Grandma's whitening bones in the top drawer of the highboy.

"But what do you *do* in the winter?" another incredulous guest asks, swabbing up the last of a four-quart casserole of beef stew and eyeing the second homemade pie possessively. "Don't you yearn to be out on the slopes?"

No, I don't but I hope she does.

I like herringbone in a suit, a snowplow on a highway, and

wax on a kitchen floor. Everything in its place, and mine is on the heated side of the window. Even if I didn't prefer it that way, I have no choice because that's where I do what I do in the winter.

Let me give you an example of what used to happen before we learned to be wary of skullduggery and crossed ski poles. After galloping through the daily chores of vacuuming, ironing, baking a couple of pies, feeding and watering the chickens, pigs, sheep and horse, I was typing an article near the phone and unfortunately picked it up before it stopped ringing. The unfamiliar voice was that of good old Jim Rickenbacker, whom we hadn't heard from in fifteen years. He and his wife, three little boys and a dog, all of whom we had never met, were planning a skiing vacation in our neck of the woods. Innocent as I still was, I suggested that they stop by on their way to Stowe. I should never have used the word stop. Not two days later they drove into our yard at nightfall, after we had finished dinner, and made it quite plain that our mountain air had given them ravenous appetites.

When I murmured that we had just finished dinner, the resourceful mother flung wide our kitchen cabinets and proudly announced that her boys weren't at all finicky. One would settle for two cans of beans, another for spaghetti, and a few cans of soup would stay the third, with tuna fish to fill in the chinks. The dog, it appeared, was a bit more choosy though equally outsized. She had thoughtfully brought a small can of dog food which she handed to me instead of shaking hands, and if we happened to have a large economy size box of corn flakes and a quart of milk, he'd be glad to slop it all over the kitchen floor.

With their supper and a week's supply of groceries disposed of, I rudely stated that we simply did not have enough beds to put them up, but that I would gladly call the nearest

112

motel for them. She was already upstairs, clomping through the bedrooms in her brand new ski boots, calling down victoriously that I needn't go to the trouble of a phone call. She had the problem solved. Hers, perhaps, not ours. With dollar signs flashing below her lowered blue eyelids, she was able to see how we could put our two daughters' mattresses on the floor in one room and bed down the boys on this king-sized pallet. Needless to say our girls had not been consulted, and their glances crackled around my aching head like sabres. When her husband announced that their dog, who always slept indoors, could be made reasonably comfortable in our bedroom, I ventured to comment that, in that case, George and I would sleep on the couch in the living room. I assumed my caustic tone would eat into her veneer, but not at all! She agreed wholeheartedly with that suggestion inasmuch as "dear old George" had to get up early to go to work.

It was not until George and I were kneading the couch pillows and struggling to swaddle ourselves somehow in the tag ends of old quilts and beach blankets, that we had a chance to plan our counterattack. We knew with awful certainty that this was no one night stand. These people had a vacation ahead of them and were determined to spend it as economically as possible, with us. We had been flattened by their steamroller approach, but we must rally our forces. Ethan Allen's ghost strode about the room reminding us that we were not the first Vermonters threatened by New Yorkers. Sometime before dawn our plans were completed. We would announce at breakfast that we were expecting other guests that afternoon. If proof were needed, a secretary in George's office and her husband, who still had the Indiana plates on his car, would drive out laden with skis and empty suitcases.

It worked. In fact with wholehearted support from the girls, we talked up the imminent arrival of Jody and Fritz sufficiently to dislodge the Rickenbackers before lunch. I gaily made them a tower of sandwiches for the road. They also took a carton of cigarettes, bottles of Coca-Cola and four cans of dog food on their own initiative.

Of course, all our snowbound days aren't that hectic. Some days all I have to do besides exchanging bamboo ski poles for Fiberglas ones and squaretoed boots for roundtoed ones, waiting for new bindings to be put on old skis or old bindings to be put on new skis, listening to the weather report and admiring blisters, is relax in front of the fire. I admire my lovely unfractured legs and address a huge pile of funny ski cards to our friends in traction. When I run out of those elongated comic cards, I answer letters from long-forgotten "friends" who are thinking of coming up our way for a week-end of skiing. It's easy now. I have a form letter.

It reads: "Darling Midge, Boots, or Puss, George and I are ecstatic to learn that you now have eight children on skis, and that we shall catch a glimpse of you over Washington's Birthday. It will be only a glimpse, however, and it will be at the first interchange on the New York Throughway. We will spend the weekend in your apartment to save money for The Four Seasons and "What Makes Sammy Run?" while you dry your ski socks in front of our fire. Directions to the liquor and grocery stores are scotch-taped to the stove. Do bring the children, your own sheets and towels and cigarettes. Ski Heil, and don't forget the key to your apartment!"

A Country Wife's
Views on Security

WHEN I was a little girl we used to amuse ourselves by re-
peating a word over and over again until it lost its meaning.
The same thing happens gradually when a word is used too
frequently in our conversation and writing. *Security* has been
overworked recently. A chill, crisp word it is for something
whose essence should be warmth and understanding. "Gilt-
edged" pops in front of it as a suitably metallic and sharp
adjective for this brittle word. It has become brittle in meaning as well as in sound because a great deal of the talk about
security concerns itself with financial arrangements and in-
surance against future threats, from broken bones to inter-
national treaties. But the people who pursue security find
it an elusive quarry. True security is not a commodity to be
bought or won in the future. It is a present state of mind, a
satisfaction in being who you are, where you are and with
whom you are, even if you are alone. Perhaps especially
when you are alone.

In our accelerated craving for "togetherness" and belonging, we have shattered security into a thousand fragments
that have no pattern. It is impossible to get to know anyone
at a cocktail party because you are jammed and jostled in
such proximity, your hands immobilized by a glass and a
potato chip with a precarious load of dip, and deafened by
such a babble of words that communication is out of the
question.

The function of a family room, if there is one, might be
primarily as a place where some of the noise and confusion

117

of family life can be isolated so that one or two members of the family can find security in another part of the house. The times when "togetherness" pervades our household are when each member of the family is happily engrossed in the pursuit of his own work in a separate room with pleasant awareness that he is adjacent to but not invaded by other satisfying activities.

What a sense of security we get from the lines,

> *Twas the night before Christmas, and all through*
> *the house*
> *Not a creature was stirring, not even a mouse.*

No one was stirring! There had been activity and there would be again, but the isthmus of silence between commotions, the feeling of warmth indoors on that cold night, and the unspoken awareness of people loving and loved, enabled Clement Moore to describe security.

Elizabeth Coatsworth, in her book *Maine Ways,* tells of waking in her farmhouse bedroom on a winter morning. "The windows are furred with a white hoar frost nearly half an inch thick, through which the morning light shines strangely. If a glass of water has been left on the table beside the bed, it is crusted with ice. And yet I am warm between feather bed and blankets, warm with a peculiar felicity. To be warm in a warm room is nothing; but to be warm in an icily cold room is to taste a very special pleasure, a security in danger, peace in a storm." And later, "Certainly we are out of touch with the world here in snow time. But many of our happiest memories are winter memories. Each day is a sort of triumph. It takes so much effort and planning merely to exist and keep warm. But see, we have been comfortable, we have been content! And each night we go to our beds with a sense of having truly lived that day."

A Country Wife's Views on Security

Perhaps it is easier to be on familiar terms with security in the country. Surrounded by ever-changing weather and compelled by necessity to do more things for themselves than city dwellers, most country people feel togetherness without having to build a room for it. I look across our snowy fields at night through the great Gothic arches of our elm trees and see the tiny squares of light in the windows of our neighbors' house. We may not see each other for weeks at a time, but if our car gets stuck in the drifted snow of our lane, our neighbor and his tractor are there before I've had time to wallow back to the house for a shovel. We are comforted by their lights and the frail plume of smoke drifting from their chimney, and they by ours. There is no need to say, "We must get together sometime soon." We know we will, quite naturally, either to share some burden or pleasure.

Irksome and frustrating as farm chores may be, the very frustrations seem to underline the pleasure of accomplishment and draw a circle around some little event making it a cherished memory. I have been near tears, chasing a small pig, my throat burning and my legs aching, but when the foolish little slippery pig was finally caught and carried shrieking back to the pen, my pleasure in hearing him grunt and snuffle once more in the shavings has been enhanced by the chase. Each morning when I feed the chickens I dread stuffing myself into the tattered old coat, the ridiculous hunting cap and heavy mittens. But after I have scattered the scratch grain, gathered the eggs, poured out the mash and filled the waterers to the brim, my cup, too, runneth over.

Security may be found in the city of course—wherever there are people, there will inevitably be some channels of communication—but it is more the exception than the rule.

One wonderful exception I remember happened when our

119

Life Up-Country

older daughter was two years old. She had an old "Sleepy Doll," a saggy nondescript rag which to her was that strange symbol of security often cherished by a small child. Patty and I, returning one day from a foray into the wilds of Central Park, discovered that Goggy was no longer with us. The bus from which we had just alighted was pulling away, but its number was clearly visible. Patty was inconsolable so I asked the next bus driver how long it would take the bus to go across town and make the return trip to our corner. When we found it would be forty minutes we went home, had lunch and came back to our rendezvous with high hopes. Curiously we both believed that Goggy would come back. When bus number 5642 hove in sight we were there, and drooping over the driver's wheel in all her faded glory, was Goggy.

"I knew you'd be here," the driver grinned sheepishly, handing down Goggy. "My kid had one of them things, only it was a piece of blanket."

Robert Frost tells of this empathy in his "Tuft of Flowers."

And feel a spirit kindred to my own;
So that henceforth I worked no more alone;

And then I remembered the concluding lines of that lovely poem.

"Men work together," I told him from the heart,
"Whether they work together or apart."

This sort of togetherness, the crystallized moment of harmony between yourself and your surroundings, this awareness of belonging—now, here—returns the meaning and warmth to a word drained of its vitality.

120

Pieces of Eight,
Too Nice to Use

THIS morning when I was straightening the linen closet, I came upon some embroidered pillowcases which my mother would have called "too nice to use." Does anyone say that anymore? As a child I remember that most of my grandmother's lares and penates were "too nice to use"; the Baleek tea set, the Paisley shawl, the horsehair love seat, and the complete sets of Emerson and Hawthorne, all were out of bounds. Perhaps if I had gone west with a schoolteacher husband and six small children I too might have hoarded my proof of Victorian status, but my mother had two daughters and she also stored up riches which might as well have been in heaven. The best china was used not more than three times a year. I wasn't allowed to wash it or even stack the dishes, which was their only merit in my eyes. The good silver, which meant sterling, was used only for ladies' teas and special company dinners during the fifty-six years of her marriage.

Her linen closet actually contained linen, Irish linen damask tablecloths with napkins big enough to be card table covers, drawn-work tea cloths with their lace Valentine napkins and sheets and pillowcases encrusted with tatting that never reclined on a bed. They were folded tenderly and stacked like ingots of gold at Fort Knox. My mother never got off the linen standard. In her later years when I once hinted that our sheets were disintegrating and that I would be very happy to have some of her unused second-best sheets for Christmas, she bought me new ones, explaining that she liked to know hers were *there* so that she would always have something nice if she needed it. As for herself, like the Boston ladies and their hats, she didn't buy sheets, she *had* them.

But there is one historic lag from that era—guest towels, probably the most studiously avoided item in any bathroom. They did and do get a fair amount of wear and tear making the round trip from linen closet to towel rack but never, to the best of my knowledge, has one been used. Frothy and frilly, abrasive with monograms or slick and as unabsorbent as waxed paper, their appearance is only ornamental and heraldic, like the royal standard at Windsor Castle flown when the Queen is in residence. The guest towel in the bathroom proclaims to apprehensive children and husbands that a guest has been, is, or will shortly be making an appearance. A guest will dry his hands on a hidden corner of a bath towel, dab at them with toilet paper or rub them together over the radiator sooner than sully these sacramental cloths. Once when I put flowered paper towels right next to the wash basin, the habit of generations was so strong that two guests gingerly used the paper towels and then smoothed out the wrinkles, folded them neatly and replaced them on top of the pile.

There is a rift in most families as divisive as the San Andreas fault. I am not a hoarder. Neither is Patty. But I am married to one and he has passed those genes on to Debbie. To look in her room you would think he had passed on to her everything else he had ever owned, too. Her desk and closet suffer from chronic accretion and George saves everything from peanut butter jars to the Boy Scout pants he last wore in 1928. Patty and I are frequently in what the other two refer to as "the throws." But even I found it wrenching to dispose of those enormous outdated tablecloths and I still have my mother's doily case full of assorted real lace, not because I have any use for it, but because one doesn't put the crown jewels on the auction block.

How can something be too nice to use? If you cherish it it should be part of your daily life. We used our solid silver from the day we were married until it was stolen thirty years later. We have a small house now and all our little *objets d'amour* are where we can see and touch them daily. Their value is more in association than in money. They have been collected or given to us over the years and each one has a story—the copper dipper made by Dave Gallup of Underhill and brought to us by Ed Andrews when we were in temporary exile from Vermont. The drawing of leaves Patty did for us one Christmas, the painting of the Jericho red mill that Gerry Miller painted in Kansas as a surprise for us, the mobile Debbie made from the shells of horseshoe crabs, black and gold flower plaques sent from a doctor in Vietnam, the girls' battered silver cups, dimpled from imperious pounding on high-chair trays, the etching of Robert Frost that Lou Calisti found for us when we left Boston. Most of these were we'll-miss-you-when-you-go presents or thank-you gifts. We cherish them for their own beauty and because we like to be surrounded by the friends who chose them for us. They are not "too nice to use." The doll that was too good to play with in my childhood was never loved. I never hugged her, shook her or confided my small grievances in her bisque ear. She has lasted through the years in my sister's attic, but she never lived. It was a squashed-nosed, nondescript rag of a doll who shared the long bittersweet years of my childhood.

In Old Vermont

Treasure in Our Attic

WE knew we were lucky to find the old white farmhouse in South Burlington. Our "winter dwelling place," as it is called in the early deeds, was simple, with the foursquare, unadorned architecture whose beauty arises from its honesty of purpose. But along with the massive stone foundation, the rough adzed beams, and wide floorboards, we inherited a family of ghosts starting with John Fay, who built the house in 1808, and continuing to his great-grandson Lynn Tracy who traveled halfway across the continent to help me pull together the drawstring on our purse of inherited tradition.

We didn't know we had treasure in our attic. In fact our attic was almost inaccessible. The only reason we crawled through the trapdoor to examine its dark recesses in the first place was because we decided to insulate.

My husband, armed with a lamp on an extension cord and bags of insulation, crept along the narrow plank which spanned the old joists, cautious lest he step off and crash through the ceiling in an upstairs bedroom. His muffled voice called down, "Bring me a bushel basket. There are a lot of old papers and junk between the joists."

Subsequently he lowered a basket full of rags, old newspapers, chunky diaries and a collection of yellowed letters covered with a fine layer of black dust. I brushed one off, sneezed, and glanced at the date written in the embellished penmanship of long ago. September 12, 1792. I collapsed on the floor, snatched up another letter and brushed off the dust. April 25, 1801. I shouted up to George who scrambled down, and all efforts at insulation were temporarily abandoned.

In Old Vermont

The newspapers spanned the period from 1817 to 1860. The letters were earlier, from 1789 to 1809. Neighbors knew little about our house farther back than the turn of the century. The town clerk's records started in 1865 when South Burlington became a separate town from Burlington. All of these letters were written to or by John Fay, but the only name which meant anything to us was that of Dr. Jonas Fay, who was a physician, the author of Vermont's Declaration of Independence, and a member of the Council of Safety that was organized in 1777 as an interim government to protect Revolutionary Vermont against the British.

At first it took nearly half an hour to decipher each letter, and the lack of continuity and the pressure of getting on with the insulation forced me to set aside the letters with the thought that some rainy day I would arrange them in chronological order and read them all. It was not until I read John Fay's words to Dr. Jonas Fay that I began to feel a certain obligation to our dusty legacy. "The invention of writing may be considered an invaluable blessing to civilized society. Without it posterity could profit but very little from the experience of their ancestors." What had been the experiences of this man one hundred and sixty years ago, and what did they mean to us living in his house?

A few months later Lynn Tracy appeared at our door. With this propitious visit the pieces of our puzzle snapped into position. Mr. Tracy was able to supply us with facts, anecdotes, and wonderful written reminiscences of his ancestors, who shared John Fay's enthusiasm for recording reactions to experiences. I climbed the wobbly ladders in the City Hall archives and tapped the resources of the Bennington Museum and the Vermont Historical Society.

Vermont is a small state but there is nothing small in its tradition of freedom. In a time when independence of

128

thought and the dignity of the individual are threatened by forces incompatible with the democratic way of life, I am thankful that our children have lived in a house rich in Vermont heritage.

In the concluding paragraph of her book *Vermont Tradition,* Dorothy Canfield Fisher says:

"Anyone who has been part of such solidarity, not as an ideal, a theory, something in a book, a spiritual aspiration, but as a living fiber in everybody's heart—he knows that we have a chance. A fighting chance. Enough. What more is needed for any heart with courage in it?"

And this is the treasure we found in our attic.

John Fay of Burlington

✠✠

Rich man, poor man, beggar man, thief
Doctor, lawyer, merchant, chief.

THE first line of this jingle is singularly applicable to France and England of 1800 with their extremes of wealth and poverty, their masses begging for food and their self-indulgent rulers stealing from them for the luxuries of court life.

And the second line was true of North America and especially New England in 1800. There were some moderately rich men and some moderately poor. Often a man was alternately rich and poor. But there were no beggar men. Jefferson wrote, "I never yet saw a native American begging in the streets or highways. . . . We have no paupers."

Doctors, lawyers, merchants, chiefs were also farmers. Nine tenths of the legislators were farmers. And in the United States of 1800 farming and learning went together. Van Wyck Brooks tells us, "It was a New Jersey farmer, as Thomas Jefferson pointed out, who invented the modern wagon wheel, of which he had found an exact description in Homer. American farmers, . . . Jefferson added, were the only farmers who could read Homer."

Where in the world but here could you find landowners who farmed themselves, who were well educated, who had read law under Cabinet members, who had money invested in ships that sailed from New York to Cadiz and the Indies, and who had commissions in the Army as well as memories of the Revolutionary War?

As early as 1766, Connecticut and Massachusetts were too binding in thought and space for the men who pushed up into Vermont. Such a man was Stephen Fay who moved his family in that year from Hardwick, Massachusetts, to Bennington, Vermont. His Catamount Tavern became the meeting place for these restless, intelligent, independent men who formed their own opinions on every subject from Holland gin to political issues. Five of Stephen's seven sons fought in the Revolutionary Battle of Bennington, and a sixth, Jonas, directed the scouts from the council chamber on the second floor of the Tavern. Jonas was a doctor; David a lawyer; Joseph a merchant; and all of them were soldiers.

Stephen's son John, father of "our" John, was the first American killed that August day of the Battle of Bennington. He was forty-three years old and doubtless his nine-year-old son John had eluded his mother's watchful eye and was with his uncle Jonas at the Tavern, more proud than sad to be the son of a hero. It was an exciting life for a boy in Bennington at that time. As he stumbled behind the plow in the spring he began to yearn for fields of his own. Spring probably called him also to the rushing streams and still pools for trout and into the woods with his father's gun for squirrel, deer and even bear. From his uncle David, the lawyer, John Fay absorbed an interest in explicit phrases and careful records. As he jogged over the rutted roads on house calls with his uncle Jonas, he caught Dr. Fay's vigorous and humorous understanding of the rights of man as an individual and as a part of a large community. Stopping for supper at Dr. Fay's house, he may have pumped water for his cousin, Susannah. At his grandfather's tavern, rubbing down the glistening horses of the mail riders, and listening to the tales of barter, he became shrewd in evaluating a trick and resentful of tricks played on him. He wanted to know more of legal procedure and books. In 1790 he was at Yale. Though the city was novel to him, he must have felt at home in a college led by Ezra Stiles, whose love of democracy, Jefferson and the

In Old Vermont

French were the loyalties John had learned in Vermont along with violent dislike for the Tories.

But he wanted to take his own part in the affairs of men. Connecticut was becoming predominantly Federalist and many there yearned to be back under English rule. The independence and the mountains of Vermont pulled him back to Bennington and then to Burlington.

His laundry lists and boarding bills tell us that he lived at the Bay, which was the local term for the cluster of houses at the edge of Lake Champlain. He practiced law, tried his hand at storekeeping "and found it not to my taste," and bought land when he could afford it. The mail brought news from home to a lonely young man so he sought the company of the riders and soon became postmaster. Trips to Bennington were heartwarming and he renewed his spirited tussles with his cousin Susannah. In 1796 he wrote his uncle David, "I have now to tell you in truth that I am married to cousin Sukey," [Susannah] and continues, "I dare say you have heard many shocking things about me since my return from Bennington. My duelling. . . . I shall observe that I was much determined to end the days of several . . . or finish my own. . . . But as fate would have it no lives have been lost. . . . To tell the truth we have a D—nd Nincompoop Court in this country and as for the hog of a Dutch judge, I will break his infernal skull except he both repents and reforms."

John wrote weekly to his uncle, Col. Joseph Fay, the merchant in New York who had gone with Ira Allen to discuss a Union of Vermont with Canada in the so-called "Haldimand negotiations" during the Revolution. Through these letters, sometimes in flowery extravagant phrases, sometimes in angry abbreviated lines, these men communicated the wide range of their thoughts and emotions. When Col. Joseph

132

journeyed to Philadelphia by stage in 1798 he wrote, "I spent two days in Philadelphia, attended Congress, the Senate in many of their interesting debates, visited and had a long conversation with Mr. Jefferson. I attended the Theatre, the best in the country, visited the prisons and other public places, found myself surrounded by an indescriminate crowd of all classes. . . . I proceded to partake of all the natural and agreable enjoyments of the Capital. The great current of public clammer is the Natural consequence of a dying spirit which has gone forth among the people and which I doubt will break on their own disordered and Devoted heads, to serve the private interest of a few . . . Bankrupts and speculators who will be the last to fight or pay the bill."

John's cousin, Joseph, son of Col. Joseph, who was studying law in Col. Alexander Hamilton's office in New York, spent many months visiting John in Burlington and wanted "very much to fix my residence in Burlington where I can be surrounded by you all . . . free from corrupt society and smoke and in the midst of some of the wildest, handsomest scenes nature ever formed." But his father's death the next year kept him in New York, always yearning to return to Vermont.

These men were very close to the Green Mountain Boys. John's father and uncles had fought with Ethan Allen and knew him well. Mrs. Ira Allen, Ethan's sister-in-law, "watched" John Fay's daughter when she was ill. Col. Joseph Fay wrote his son, who was visting in Burlington, "I hope you will call and see Mrs. Penniman (Ethan Allen's widow) and the young Ethans, the old general was truly my friend and worthy of my best remembrance."

The hardheaded and sometimes ruthless ways of the Green Mountain Boys were being tempered by men like "our" John Fay, who, while hotheaded in personal matters, craved law and order in the developing state. His tireless efforts as a lawyer in Burlington were for just settlement of land claims, and in his legal notes he repeatedly urged absentee owners to come to Vermont and settle on their land. His time seems to have been spent as much in the buying and selling of land as in the practice of law.

He had been a poor man and a moderately rich man, a lawyer, merchant and chief and might have served his state more illustriously in later life had not tuberculosis been such a common scourge. His letters from 1804 to 1808 refer to asthma and coughing blood with increasing frequency. He died in 1809 and was buried first on his land northwest of the college green at the University of Vermont; later he was moved to the Eldredge Cemetery adjoining the present Burlington Airport, where the air turbulence of the jet planes shivers through the grass on his grave.

The Daughter of
Dr. Jonas Fay

FOR many years historians were more concerned with the
dates of battles than with the forces which motivated the
men who fought them. Yet from Hannibal to Hitler, individual personalities have been magnetic enough to change
the course of history.

In Vermont's early years, Ethan Allen had this magnetic
quality. His actual accomplishments, compared to the years
of diplomatic service of his brother Ira, were negligible, but
his personality became a symbol, a flame, and the essence of
the determination of every settler in the New Hampshire
Grants, as Vermont was called in his time. We have no picture or accurate description of Ethan Allen's appearance, yet
his personality was so distinctive that it has assumed physical form.

Some of these vibrant people convey their essential quality through their letters or diaries, some from the anecdotes
and legends that surround them. One of the greatest pleas-
ures derived from historical research is the gradual emer-
gence of a little-known person from misty obscurity into
living color.

One daughter of the Revolution lived in our South Burlington house for more than half a century, Susannah Fay.
Although none of the letters and diaries found in our attic
was written by her, Susannah, through anecdote and refer-
ence, steps briskly from the yellowed pages, more alive than
many of her relatives. The women in Revolutionary Vermont

rarely were active in public life. But they worked as hard as the men and usually outlived them. Their daily courage and zest for life becomes heroic if judged by present standards.

Susannah, the daughter of Sarah Fasset and Dr. Jonas Fay, was born in Bennington on October 2, 1769. When she was three years old her father and grandfather were sent as agents for the Grants to lay citizens' complaints before Governor Tryon of New York. She was five years old when her father was surgeon under Ethan Allen at Ticonderoga. Before she was eight years old her father had written Vermont's Declaration of Independence. On an August day of the same year, 1777, Susannah, or Sukey as she was called, stood with her brother and sisters on the Bennington village green and waved the militia off to the famous battle of Walloomsac.

All that day Sukey folded bits of linen for bandages and ran back and forth to her Aunt Mary Robinson's house where great iron pots of stew were simmering for the soldiers. Aunt Mary Fay Robinson was the wife of Moses Robinson, who later became Governor. There was plenty of work and excitement for an eight-year-old girl. Children may have been seen and not heard but Sukey did a good deal of listening as well as looking. She heard the distant rumble of guns all through the long muggy afternoon. She heard the scout shouting, "Victory is ours," as he galloped up Bennington hill at sunset. She saw the lines of bedraggled prisoners led past her grandfather's tavern, to be bound with ropes she and her sisters had hastily untied from their bedsteads. She saw her grandfather's face when he was told that his oldest son had been killed, and she heard him say, "I am proud that I had a son willing to give his life for his country."

A week after John Fay was shot, his two-year-old son died. The next week his widow died and the following week his five-year-old son. It is probable that young John Fay, a year older than his cousin Sukey, orphaned and bereaved, was taken in by his father's brothers, Jonas and Joseph, and that Sukey and John grew up together unaware that they would be married before the turn of the century.

It is possible that spirited little Sukey did a great deal to alleviate the tragedies in John's childhood. Ethan Allen had returned from prison in England and was swashbuckling about the Catamount Tavern once more, to Sukey's delight and admiration. That Sukey was gay and daring we know from an anecdote written by her granddaughter, Susan Elizabeth Fay Tracy, to her son Lynn Tracy in 1921.

"Haven't I told you that Ethan Allen and my grandmother were friends? They attended singing school together, and once when grandmother was not present he jumped on his horse and went after her. He says, 'We can't sing without Susannah Fay' and she jumps on the horse behind him and rides to singing school."

The picture of Sukey in her late teens, her hooded cloak sailing out behind her, clinging to the great bulk of Ethan Allen as they galloped through the night, is very appealing.

Apparently Sukey spent as much time as possible on horseback. Her granddaughter, Caroline Fay Kimball, writes, "She was tall, straight and strong and was a fine rider. To see her and my mother ride made me early want to learn. . . . My grandmother used to tell me how she went to church riding on a pillion behind her husband carrying a foot stove with coals in it to keep the feet warm, as they had no stoves in churches in those days."

Sukey married "our" John in 1796. There were some objections because of their "affinity," as cousins, and for some reason John felt called upon to fight a duel at this time, but no one was killed and John and Sukey came to live in Burlington, where John had been the first postmaster for four years. They lived on the northwest corner of Pearl and North Prospect Streets, known then as "the road leading past Col. Pearl's dwelling to the Bay, and the road to the Intervale." In the same year, John had bought a piece of land on the present Hinesburg Road in South Burlington. In 1808 they built a house and moved to the "farm." John was afflicted with asthma, later to be recognized as tuberculosis. Perhaps they thought country living would improve his health. Unfortunately his health became worse and he died in 1809 at the age of forty-one. Sukey was forty. She had a twelve-year-old son, John Johnson Fay, and a daughter, Caroline. Another little daughter, Sukey, aged five, had been buried in Eldredge Cemetery the year before.

Death was no stranger to Sukey Fay. She bought two and a half yards of black "crape, millenet, wire and a handkerchief" from Mr. Hickok and made herself a hat for "mourning apparel." There is no mention of further widow's weeds. Her cousin, Moses Fay, as administrator of her late husband's estate, made an inventory of John Fay's extensive land holdings. He also listed every household article owned by the Fays at the time of John's death and every expense incurred by Sukey during the next four years. Neighbors were hired to cut the hay and plant the crops but she and John Johnson and Caroline continued to live on the farm, milking the cows and taking care of the chickens, horses, pigs and sheep. Young John's expense account when he was a student at the University and while he taught school, as well as a diary he kept when he was twenty-five, tell us a good deal about life in the early nineteenth century. They rode into the village to church each Sunday. They entertained a good many visiting relatives, and John Johnson and Caroline went to singing schools, dances, barn raisings and "slaying" outings several evenings a week. Hard cider and rum flowed freely but the

horses which pulled the sleighs home at night did not drink.

John Johnson Fay was a scholar and preferred his books to farming. This did not disturb Sukey. Her husband had studied law at Yale. Her father was a doctor as well as the author of many of the early state documents. In fact throughout the extensive correspondence between the members of this family, there is a breadth of vocabulary and lack of grammatical errors which contrast sharply with the rustic phrases put into the mouths of some of these same people in historical fiction. It is easy to suppose that as John Johnson became more and more absorbed in his books, Sukey took over the management of the farm.

When John married Mindwell Brewster he brought his bride home to live. Though they lived with Sukey for the next thirty-seven years, she was a wise and tender matriarch. Mindwell reigned in the kitchen. Mindwell also kept silkworms on shelves in the dining room, fed them on mulberry leaves and wound the silk into threads. Sukey became a storybook grandmother. The grandchildren liked nothing better than to hear her tell of Revolutionary Bennington. She taught them to ride horseback and took them sleighing on the snowy roads. In the evening she taught the girls how to spin and weave their home-grown flax into linen and tow cloth. Letters from uncles, cousins and grandchildren send special remembrance to Sukey.

Though gallons of rum were purchased for the hired men during haying, and though Cousin Moses Fay's wife "was burned to death when her clothes ignited from a candle held in her lap while in a state of intoxication," there is no evidence that Sukey cared much for spirits. But she did enjoy a pinch of snuff. Snuff appears frequently on the grocery lists and one of her grandchildren writes in the 1850's, when

In Old Vermont

Sukey was past eighty, "Grandmother has just opened the closet dore to get a pinch of snuff."

Perhaps it was her snuff box which indirectly caused her death at the age of ninety-three. She apparently fell from a stool while trying to reach a high shelf in the kitchen and died soon after the fall.

Her life spanned the years from the eve of the Revolution to the eve of the Civil War. The young girl and the young state grew up together into dignified maturity that merited respect. From one war for freedom to another war for freedom the worth of industry and independence was never questioned by Susannah Fay or Vermont.

Journey from Burlington to New York in 1801

☒☒

"WHENEVER I go to Vermont I feel that I am travelling toward my own place," Bernard DeVoto wrote in *Harper's*, December, 1951.

You do not have to be a Vermonter to experience this sense of returning home. The home that Vermont represents may be a dream of rural life. It may be a picture of a white church presiding over the elms on a village green. It may be the smell of woodsmoke in a farmhouse kitchen or the patches of bluets like mirages of the recent snows on rocky pastures in May. But there are few of us, no matter where we were born, who haven't felt this tingle of recognition.

In 1801, Hiram Fay, cousin of "our" John Fay, lived in New York City. His father was Col. Joseph Fay, and Hiram had sailed on his father's brigs to France, England, Spain and the Indies. He had seen a good deal of the world and was familiar with the cosmopolitan little city of New York. But something kept drawing him back to Vermont between his voyages. Returning to New York, after a visit to his cousin John, Hiram wrote:

After bidding you adieu! I rode for the most part of the day through woods, the wind roared among the trees, the leaves rattled, the craggy tops of the wavy pines sailed over our heads, the sky grew dark, the tempest roared thru the opening of the mountains and echoed along the winding of the valley. The horses startled and shivered at the blast, and even I sighed! and wished for your fireside and the sweet

*music of Collard. However I consoled myself with the idea
that it would be fair tomorrow and then the pleasure which
I should enjoy would fully compensate for the evils of today.*

*It is not the first time I assure you that I have been happy
on the prospects of tomorrow. However about 3 o'clock in
the afternoon the wind began to die away and the riding was
more agreable. We rode untill about 8 o'clock in the evening
when we came to an inn kept by a Mr. West at the distance
of 45 miles from Burlington, where we concluded to take up
our lodging. Our horses were taken care of, our suppers prepared, and I soon lodged in the sweet embrace of Morpheus.
On the ensuing morning the sun appeared to rise from behind the eastern mount with redoubled Splendor, and
though the weather was something cold, yet compared with
the former day the riding was truly delightful. I never was
more pleased than journeying through this country, the
mountains rose majestic on each side of the road, and nature
seemed to have formed it on purpose to delight and amuse
the weary traveller. The valleys are very winding and often
I would look around and find myself to appearance hemmed
in by mountains, to go forward was to ascend mountain
piled upon mountain, when I would be agreably disap-
pointed by winding around a high rock and finding myself
in a pleasing vale with here and there a little cot. The play-
ful children around the door, the little lambs which bounded
over the hillocks, the tinkling cowbell with the gentle mur-
murs of the stream which bordered the road and ran curving
through the valley, the herds which grazed along the banks
and the inaccessible mountains which appeared on both
sides produced a Melancholly yet pleasing joy in my bosom
which surpasses all the pleasure that it is in the power of
riches or splendor to bestow. At length I arrived in Royalton
where I spent a very agreable evening at Mr. Smiths the*

Journey From Burlington to New York in 1801

attorney. The time was passed away with entertaining conversation seasoned with apples whist and cider when my fancy soon ran home and found me again in Burlington. On the following day I reached Hanover. Here I remained a fortnight and passed my time very agreably in writing reading and sporting. After two weeks had passed away I mounted my horse and turned my face for home. My journey on the banks of the Connecticut was equally pleasing but time will not permit me to relate it at present. I will only observe that although the villages are handsome and the people refined, yet the scenery of that Country is far inferior, and the inhabitants not to be compared with the hardy green mountain boys or simple republicans of Vermont. When I arrived in New Haven I found my mother had gone on to New York, I therefore remained only one hour in that place, left my horse to be sold, and embarked on board Packet at 9 o'clock in the evening and arrived in New York the next morning at ten. So ends my short sketch of my little journey.

Lizzie Fay, Susannah's Granddaughter

ONE hundred and five years ago, Susan Elizabeth Fay, sixteen, was awakened by her mother's remark that although it was as cold as Greenland, school kept. I thought of this one morning when I woke our sixteen-year-old Patty.

What possible common interests could be shared by these two girls who slept in the same room more than a hundred years apart? Well, just about everything that shapes the complicated, frustrating, exciting world of sixteen. School, boys, clothes, community events and even the world outside of South Burlington, Vermont, made up the colorful kaleidoscope of Lizzie's thoughts as well as Patty's.

I have no first-person record of Lizzie's reactions. If she kept a diary, it was probably as private as Patty's. But between the lines of her father's diary and the letters written by her husband to their son, invisible ink tells of a life strangely similar to that of a modern Vermont girl.

Lizzie was in the third class at the Academy in Burlington, corresponding to our sophomore year of senior high school. During part of the year her father drove her the three miles to school each morning. Sometimes her father was not able to pick her up in the afternoon and she had to walk home or find occasional ride. Part of the time she boarded at Mrs. Sarah Slocum's. But the transportation problem, then as now, had its fringe benefits. Several years before there had been one memorable ride. Wheeler Tracy (whom Lizzie married in 1867) tells about it in writing to his son, Lynn Tracy.

In 1857 my father made many improvements in our house and sent me for lime needed in making plaster. The lime kiln

146

was located two miles beyond Burlington. In a lumber wagon with empty boxes on which I sat, I was going up Pearl Street in Burlington when a woman halted me and asked if I would give a girl a ride, that the girl was bound to walk home three miles and she thought it was too much for her. Of course I was willing. Meanwhile I saw a black haired, black eyed, red cheeked little girl peeking around the corner of the house and protesting. But the woman persuaded the girl to accept the ride.

I assisted the girl to mount the box beside me. When a mile past the town an Irish woman begged a ride. She climbed up and seated herself on a box having a lid which I held down as if to avoid the escape of the contents. When we reached the woman's home and she wished to get down she would not stir until I pressed down the cover of the box. She declared I was a showman, that I could not fool her, and there must be monkeys or some kind of animal in the box.

Another mile and I had to turn to the left and the girl beside me said her home was the second house to the right. As she climbed down to the road I asked who she lived with and her face blushed scarlet as she told me the name. I forgot the name but remembered the girl.

Two years later I was teaching my first school when two girls from Burlington visited some cousins who were pupils. Each day for about ten days these visting girls were at the school. The day before they returned home one of them asked me if I knew Lizzie Fay. I replied that I had never heard of such a girl. "Well," she said, "Lizzie Fay, while boarding with us has many times described a boy who was going for lime with whom she rode mounted on a box and you exactly fit the description she gives of that boy." I replied, "Well yes, I remember the girl but not the name."

A year later I attended a Teachers' Association which was held in the Congregational Church in Burlington. I was in the gallery and in front of me was Sarah Slocum, one of the visitors at my first school. She seemed to be looking for the arrival of someone below. At last, with much effort she succeeded in getting the attention of a girl who came into the gallery and sat by her. I thought nothing of this but when there was singing this strange girl kept looking back at me. Later she told me it was then she fell in love with my tenor voice. When the meeting was over I was introduced to this Lizzie Fay and was permitted to see her home. I was invited in and spent an hour. Meanwhile as was the fashion in those days I wished on her ring.

A few weeks later Lizzie's father notes in his diary that, Mrs. Fay bought a dress for Susan (Lizzie) in the Bee Hive Store. Nothing remarkable in that item today, but we can guess what pressure had been brought to bear on her parents to buy a store dress at a time when most girls' calico and muslin frocks were made at home! And she was not unaware of the charm of her red cheeks. Another notation in her father's diary shows he had been persuaded to buy two cakes of "cast steel" soap for Lizzie for five cents.

During this year at the Academy, Lizzie took in a variety of events in Burlington. Her father enjoyed his frequent trips to town and apparently did not suspect that Lizzie accompanied him in the hopes of catching a glimpse of the Tracy boy. They attended the Congregational Church regularly. They helped Dr. Thayer with the Medical Fair. Lizzie took piano lessons. In one week they went to the Baccalaureate, the Commencement and the exhibition at the University, and to the village to see the balloon go up. They all went fishing at Shelburne pond. This, of course was during school recess. When school started again in September there was Town Meeting (September 6) and the Vermont State Fair a week later. Lizzie had her "likeness taken" and her father purchased "bonnett and trimmings for Elizabeth for $1.70."

There was a temperance convention that probably interested Lizzie because it was in the Congregational Church, which was well known for its choir.

Lizzie's older sister, Sarah, and husband, Charles Hartshorn, from Clinton, Wisconsin, were visiting the family and Lizzie and her fourteen-year-old brother, Freddie, "went as far as Essex Junction with them in the cars." Her father does not say so but he probably drove out to meet them in the same buggy which overturned one day when Lizzie, Mrs. Fay and Lizzie's sister, Cordelia, were driving to the village.

Lizzie went to get lime at the lime kiln with her father. She was the youngest daughter, and at the time when she was sixteen, her father was sixty-four. He apparently enjoyed her company and does not comment on the fact that she always joined him on trips to the village or the lime kiln but not to Hinesburg or Milton!

The summer of 1860 was full of events which warranted a further expense of five cents for "cast steel" soap. On July 31, Lizzie's father wrote, "Honorable Stephen Douglas arrived in town. He was received by the firing of cannon and the Band, was escorted to the Court House where he made a speech and afterwards at the American Hotel where I shook hands with him."

The same evening there was an exhibition at the Congregational Church. Hardly time to go home for chores and drive back to the village again.

On August 8, the circus and menagerie opened at 2:00 P.M. on the fairground. Only a month later, he wrote, "Myself, Cordelia, Freddie and Susan [Lizzie] went to the State Agricultural Fair and the great menagerie." Two menageries a month apart!

In Old Vermont

But the next week, "Susan to board at Mrs. Sarah Slocum's while attending the Academy."

Wheeler Tracy writes:

The following autumn (1860) I attended Williston Academy and there was a boy there by the name of Fay who went home week ends. One Friday I asked him if he was related to Lizzie Fay. He said she was his sister and I sent a brief note to her in which I told her my wish when wishing on her ring, which was that I might visit her in her home sometime. In response, the next Monday came a very cordial invitation to visit her. . . . A year later a message came to me requesting me to come to the City Hall where oysters were being served by the Congregational Church ladies. I was soon there and when she saw me come in the door those red cheeks took on a deeper hue. Her friend Alma Lyon and her fiance Mr. Walker invited us to visit a dance, we to look on, they to dance and at midnight I took her to her boarding house. . . . In October 1864 I left home to work out life's problems in the wide world. I went to Burlington . . . hired a livery rig and went to see Lizzie Fay. . . . We drove around through Winooski Falls and up a hill past Green Mountain Cemetery where stands a beautiful monument to Ethan Allen and when in front of that monument Lizzie Fay promised to love me always.

She saw me board a train bound for Springfield, Mass. and went to a friend's for the night. I arrived in Springfield at 11 P.M. with 85 cents in my pocket, and a month later she was in Baltimore as a missionary teacher of the colored children. . . . She taught one year in Baltimore and two years in Norfolk, Va. with two months vacation at her home in Burlington. I was living in Springfield, Mass. and each summer went to Vermont for two weeks. On one of these sum-

Lizzie Fay, Susannah's Granddaughter

mers I took Lizzie Fay on a ride to Stowe about 30 miles from home, and on our way back we stopped overnight in Jericho at her cousin's home.

Can this be in 1864 when we have been led to believe that chaperoned young ladies spent a good deal of their time swooning in the parlor? Not Lizzie Fay!

On her way to Vermont [her husband continues] *she stopped over one train in Springfield and I took her to a hotel for dinner. While at the table it dawned on me that in changing my clothes I had forgotten to change my pocketbook and I was penniless and had to borrow money from her to pay for the meal. After three years engagement we were married at her home in Burlington on October 17, 1867.*

They lived in Wisconsin most of their long married life. Wheeler Tracy died in 1930, when they had been married for sixty-three years, and black-haired, red-cheeked Lizzie, scarcely five feet tall, died in 1939 at the age of ninety-five. The three mile walk from the Academy in Burlington to our house in South Burlington did not perceptibly shorten her life!

Along with the charming ghost of Lizzie Fay we have inherited her very much alive son, Lynn Tracy, who with Mrs. Tracy came east to visit us and spend a night in his mother's, his grandmother's, and his great-grandmother's house. Perhaps it was only the magic of a May evening in Vermont, and the fragrant lilacs brushing against the open windows, but we thought we heard the swish of skirts as Lizzie ran up the stairs to write a note to Wheeler Tracy, or the click of metal needles as her mother, Mindwell, knit fancywork gloves from the silk she had raised in the dining room, while tall grandmother Susannah slipped over to the cupboard for a last pinch of snuff.

151

Silk in Vermont

IF silk purses could have been made out of cows' ears, there is no doubt that the production of silk in Vermont would have kept pace with dairy farming. The surprising fact is that the delicate silkworm not only survived but flourished in the rigorous climate of Vermont a century and a quarter ago.

When we learned, through the memoirs of Caroline Fay Kimball, that silkworms had been raised in our old house from 1836 until the early 1860's, many questions came to mind. Where did they get the silkworm eggs? How did they incubate them? How did they maintain the constant high temperatures which the silkworm requires? And how did they grow the white mulberry tree on which the silkworm feeds, and which is not a native of the United States? An article published in the *Proceedings* of the Vermont Historical Society of June, 1940, which contains excerpts from the diaries of Seth Shaler Arnold, answers some of these questions. We hope that further research may turn up more detailed information on this widespread but little-recorded industry in early Vermont.

So many of the settlers of Vermont came from Connecticut and Massachusetts that it is not surprising to find Vermonters were in close contact with what was going on in Connecticut. When the Society of Arts offered bounties for silkworm cocoons and raw silk, the people of New England, never loath "to turn a penny in the way of trade," sat up and took notice. There was legislation for silk bounties as early as 1732 in Connecticut and, by 1750, Governor Jonathan Law was wearing a coat and stockings of Connecticut silk.

152

An essay on silk culture was written by Reverend Jared Eliot of Killingworth, Connecticut, and his neighbor, Dr. Ezra Stiles jumped on the silken bandwagon. Mulberry seeds were spread along with the gospel when the Reverend Stiles sent packets to eighty ministers, some of whom were in Vermont and the towns on Lake Champlain. In 1788 the Reverend Stiles had become the President of Yale, and at the commencement exercises in 1789 he wore a gown made of Connecticut silk.

We know that when John Fay left Yale in 1791, his saddle bags contained fifty yards of linen cloth and a list of President Stiles's land holdings in Killingworth, requested by John's uncle, Colonel Joseph Fay. It seems more than likely that a packet of mulberry seeds was tucked inside the flyleaf of the volume of Blackstone which balanced the weight of the linen cloth.

But Vermont's silk boom was to be postponed a while longer. The internal struggles of the new state and the intermittent clashes with the British on Lake Champlain were more demanding than the silk industry.

It wasn't until after 1824, when the French imported a new mulberry tree from the Philippines, that news of a new silk craze and a mulberry tree boom traveled up the Hudson to Albany and down the lakes to Burlington. It is difficult to determine just when the silk boom started in Vermont, but we know it was widespread in the Bellows Falls area in the 1830's and 1840's.

In 1836, in our house in South Burlington, Mindwell Brewster Fay was raising silkworms in the dining room. Her daughter, Caroline Fay Kimball, wrote:

Mother kept several hundred silk worms. She had a yard wide shelf made all around the large dining room and cov-

ered with paper that was changed, and quite a garden of
mulberry trees. The leaves had to be gathered twice a day
for their breakfast and supper. I soon learned to help gather
them and feed the worms. When they wound themselves into
their cocoons it was very interesting to watch them. It took a
good many cocoons to make one thread of silk. I think they
were put into water and wound at one time and then twisted
and reeled into skeins. Mother knit gloves for grandmother
and herself. They were knit open work on the back and were
very handsome.

But where did Mindwell incubate the silkworm eggs?
Caroline doesn't tell us but we may guess it was on the back
of the stove, along with the cottage cheese and her yeast
sponge.

In Seth Shaler Arnold's diaries, we note that the worm
eggs began to hatch ten days after he took them out of the
cold cellar. Although he had planted one hundred trees in
1835 and more than a hundred in 1839, the voracious appetites of the silkworms, or the loss of trees, required purchas-
ing mulberry leaves from several neighbors in 1842, when
Reverend Arnold started in the silk business. But the Philip-
pine mulberry could not stand the winters of Long Island,
much less Vermont. Soon mulberry trees were selling at one
cent each in New York. By 1850 only two hundred and sixty
pounds of silk in cocoons were produced in Vermont and it
had dropped to tenth place in silk production. Vermont
housewives, then as now accustomed to "making do," apparently fed their silkworms on another variety of mulberry,
and continued to produce enough silk for domestic use.

Commercially, sericulture was dead in Vermont and no
further legislation appears regarding bounties. The silk stockings, mitts and caps had brought a bit of luxury to our Ver-

154

mont great-grandmothers, which they had no intention of relinquishing lightly. As late as the early 1860's, Caroline Fay Kimball's daughter Harriet used to visit her grandmother Mindwell in our house. Of the silkworms she later wrote: "We were so happy when she would let us feed them and we would stand and watch them by the hour." You may be sure that little Harriet wanted to be on hand, when after a month of feeding, the worms stopped feeding and raised their heads. That was the signal that they were ready to spin. For the next three days she would run across lots to her grandmother's house to watch the worms wind the filament, which they secreted from their mouth-parts, around themselves in figure-eight motions of their heads until they were completely enclosed.

The silk craze had swept through the state and had almost disappeared twenty-five years earlier. But trees and people seem to live longer and more quietly in Vermont. This was apparently true of silkworm culture as well.

I doubt if there is a farmhouse in Vermont today, where the soft sound of the silkworms eating, like the falling of light rain on leaves, can be heard. Yet, up under the eaves in the dark attics of these houses, a yellowed pair of gloves, an unfinished stocking, or a skein of silk may be found at the bottom of many old high-topped trunks.

Thanksgiving Long Ago

OUR white farmhouse sighed a little on Thanksgiving Eve, bracing itself against the cold south wind which had swept rain and snow against its sides for over a century and a half. But there was no sadness in the sigh, just a deep breath after a job well done. In the blackened fireplace, birch logs fell apart and settled into glowing embers, while the house remembered the long succession of Thanksgiving Eves that it had sheltered.

Was that swish a curled elm leaf slapped against the shingles, or was it the rustle of skirts as Susannah Fay set the cherry table for the first Thanksgiving in this house in 1808?

The light from her homemade candles glowed softly on the pewter plates, her six silver tablespoons, twelve silver teaspoons, and a pair of silver candlesticks which she had brought from her father's house on the Blue Hill in Bennington. All her cooking would be done tomorrow at the spacious hearth, where the spit thrust out a strong black arm to hold the goose. Mincemeat stood ready in a crockery bowl and Susannah poured a little rum over the spicy mixture. There was cornmeal measured for the johnnycake, turnips and potatoes in the cellar, nuts from the butternut tree and apples to be roasted over the coals.

Susannah wiped her hands on her apron, picked up the pewter candlestick, and, shielding its flickering flame, climbed softly up the narrow stairs to see that twelve-year-old John and Sarah were snug in their featherbeds.

The house once more was silent, and the log tumbled and sent up a fountain of bright sparks.

Thirty years passed and Susannah walked across the room to get a pinch of snuff from the cupboard. A tall erect woman of seventy, in her tight-fitting black gown, she moved with dignity and grace.

But the burden of tomorrow's feast no longer rested on her shoulders. Her daughter-in-law, Mindwell, and her granddaughter, Caroline, hustled from pantry to kitchen. Caroline's own words tell us about this Thanksgiving.

My father and mother used to do a great deal to make Thanksgiving day one of the pleasantest of the year. All the absent children were expected to be there and we all lotted much on being a reunited family, and I remember mother, for some years had two or three poor people that she invited so as to make the day a happy one for them.

Every year we used to make cider applesauce a week or two before Thanksgiving, a half barrel of it to freeze for the winter. Those were very busy days; so many kinds of pies and puddings.

I remember when mother used to make a dozen or fifteen mince pies and freeze them, but later she made a large quantity of mince meat and froze it, then thawed it out as she wanted it. How we children used to like to go to the pantry and count the different kinds of pies, mince, apple and pumpkin; three kinds of pudding, one large baked Indian pudding in a six quart pan; a rice pudding in a four quart dish, and a cracker pudding for the center of the table. The large puddings were placed at the ends of the table and plenty of pies scattered all around.

We raised geese, so always had a goose roasted in a baker before the fireplace. It could be easily turned.

In Old Vermont

The image of that old baker faded, and as I watched the coals darken, another twenty years slipped by. It was 1858. The spit and the baker were no longer on the hearth. Tomorrow's goose stood guard as always in the pantry above the rows of pies, but it would be cooked in the large black wood stove in the kitchen. The pewter plates now graced the whatnot and the table was set with china. There was the rhythmic click of a rocking-chair and near the hearth, Susannah, still straight and smiling at ninety, knitted the strands of home-grown silk into gloves. Only three children lived at home now but Caroline and her husband lived near by and would walk across the brittle fields tomorrow, bringing a haunch of venison and a jar of currant jelly for the feast. Susannah sang softly to herself in a thin echo of the clear sweet voice that had joined with Ethan Allen's in the singing school in Bennington. Tomorrow would be her fiftieth Thanksgiving in this house, and for nearly as many years her husband had been buried in the little Eldredge Cemetery nearby. She folded her knitting and walked slowly to the stairs. The children upstairs now were her youngest grandchildren.

There have been other children who slept here in the last hundred years, though none of them left us records of their Thanksgivings.

The old house sighed again and settled with the cold. The fire was nearly burned out. My husband knocked apart the coals and flicked off the lamp. We had no tallow candle to carry up the stairs. But as we stood for a moment at the front window and our eyes swept up the great arch of the elm etched against the moonbright sky, we felt the nearness of our beloved ghosts.

The next day's turkey would be baked in an electric oven, but we had raised it ourselves. We had picked the apples for

158

the pies from the Northern Spy tree in the pasture. We had planted the onions and the pumpkins and fed the pigs for the sausage meat and the lard in the pie crust. We have kept faith too, Susannah, and as we silently went up the same worn steep stairs, and tucked the covers around our sleeping children, we knew again the meaning of Thanksgiving.

Good-bye and Keep Cold  VI

Little Gray Home
on the Interstate

I HAVE nothing against progress. I'm tickled to death with indoor plumbing and have long since signed a truce with the Dispos-All. But when we bought a farmhouse and ninety acres in Vermont "to have and hold," we were naive enough to think that those words meant what they said.

I've had enough experience with country roads in the mud season, and in the ice season, and in the hot season (which comes on the first Thursday in July on alternate years), to know that interstate highways represent progress. They are smooth, fast and scenic. The only trouble was that we didn't count on our most personal habits becoming part of the scenery. Protected by all that acreage, it never occurred to us that the Interstate would see fit to cut our land neatly in half and miss the house by a scant puff of carbon monoxide.

A direct hit would have emptied the house but filled the wallet. The near miss changed the character of the house and threatened to empty the wallet.

Besides, we had a sentimental attachment to our one-hundred-and-fifty year-old house, built by the son and namesake of the first American soldier killed at the Battle of Bennington. We decided to turn our bad ears toward the throughway, plant every quick growing hedge in the *Sunday Times* garden section ads, and stay put.

That's what we decided when the threat of the highway became an impending reality. But somewhat later, when our meadows were crawling with soil borers, surveyors, and highway engineers, my husband was appointed to a new job two hundred miles away. We were forced to put our house

163

Good-bye and Keep Cold

on the market willy-nilly, and from then on it was all nilly. What prospective buyers would believe that our move was purely coincidental with the approach of oversized wheels which ground slowly towards our house? Very few.

According to the samplers in our attic, the world used to be full of people just tripping over their high button shoes in their eagerness "to live by the side of the road and be a friend to man." But our brief venture into real estate soon showed us that this good was oft interred with their bones. The prospective buyer wants to be a friend allright. He enjoys studying the maps, measuring the rooms, and wasting a whole Saturday afternoon with you, but the road he hankers to live beside is not the Interstate.

We bought the house because it was historic and charming, convenient and cheap. Nine years and five thousand dollars worth of improvements later, we sold the house for the same reasons. It was still historic, still charming, still convenient, and, thanks to the throughway, cheaper than when we bought it.

I suppose real estate dealers already have statistics on the proportion of serious buyers to the casual shoppers. If they don't, I'll lend them mine. In fact I'll give them to them. In two months fifty families wiped their big and little feet on our red carpet. And the term "family" no longer is restricted to Papa Bear, Mama Bear, Baby Bear and Goldilocks. The average couple brought with them another couple, one mother-in-law, two children who could, and did, explore independently, one who could, and did, reach ashtrays, lamps and potted plants, and one who was only a bulge under the lady's hatching jacket. Another common appendage was the dear old building contractor friend, who came armed with a screwdriver, jackknife or battering ram to test the beams in the cellar. I'll admit one or two spots in our old beams were

164

a little soft to begin with, but the sound areas soon were honeycombed with the borings of these oversized termites. Of the fifty families, ten were interested and four made offers.

One lady spent a full hour poring over the Interstate maps, another hour inspecting the house, and a third denouncing its faults. When she finally rose to go, she smiled graciously and said, "I'm going to tell you a little secret, dear. I'm not interested in houses but I couldn't think *what* to do this afternoon."

Our taste in wallpaper was criticized so often that I began to suspect that I was colorblind. If I tried to conceal the wide floorboards upstairs with scatter rugs, that day's invading army said it was a crime to cover an inch of those sweet old floors. If I took the opposite tack the next day and pointed out the hand-hewn beams in the cellar, our visitors would shudder and announce that they'd never be able to sleep a wink in such an antique shelter. But the final blow was delivered by a buxom matron in stretch pants pressed into service far beyond the call of duty. Her eyes swept up and down our long sunny living room and dining area.

"No dining room?" she gasped. "It may be all right for *you* to picnic but when we entertain, our guests are always important people!"

I remembered the college presidents, the senators, the writers, doctors and artists who had "picnicked" in this room, their digestions apparently unhindered by the absence of protocol. Oh well, she wouldn't have been happy in our house anyway. The ghost of Susannah, the first mistress of the house, would have haunted her soirées.

For two months I folded the newspaper while it was still in front of my husband's face, scraped dishes before they were empty, and made the beds while my children were still in them. I had so many appointments with our lawyer that it would have been cheaper and less soul searching to have been psychoanalyzed. Every real estate dealer in town called me by my first name and I'm glad they never heard the names I called them.

Then one fine May morning, the highway engineer, who apparently rolled up in his blanket and slept in the fields, asked me to walk the line in the most remote corner of our land at 7:00 A.M. The beds were left unmade, the breakfast dishes were still on the table, and an unflattering caricature of a real estate agent adorned the kitchen blackboard. When I returned there was a note from that same agent beneath her portrait. She had brought a client to see the house. He loved every messy inch of it and wanted to buy our little gray home on the Interstate.

Salesmanship, they say, is being at the right place at the right time, like in the far corner of your land when the house is being shown. And if you don't own ninety acres on which to get lost, just get lost. Polish the chromium or leave the eggy dishes in the sink. Plump the pillows or throw them on the floor. It makes no difference. The only deterrent to selling a house on an interstate highway is the hard-sell glint in the owner's eye. Caveat emptor, the lawyers always say. And if the owner is so disinterested in the sale that he is tramping across the back forty, or cruising around the Bahamas, what need is there for the buyer to beware? He'll take the high road and you'll still have time to take the low road and be at the savings bank before him to sign the mortgage papers.

Good-bye and Keep Cold

✂✂

I SUPPOSE time will cure our homesickness for Vermont. It hasn't been very long since we sold our old white farmhouse whose windows looked westward to the Adirondacks and eastward to Camel's Hump and Mount Mansfield.

Only time for one frost to have curled the leaves of the pumpkins I planted last spring and lit the swamp maples at the edge of the woods. Not long enough perhaps to look back at Vermont with vision unclouded by well-remembered patterns, the incongruous contrast of sea gulls waddling awkwardly in our meadow among the crows, the blanket of mist tucked in around the edges of the lake on a cold morning, or the wedge of geese streaking across the evening sky.

Perhaps we have not been exiled long enough to see Vermont objectively, but if time be lacking, distance is not, and with increasing maturity an arm's length sharpens the focus of an image.

I have been unpacking our books this morning, arranging them on the shelves in our new house—the unread ones, the disturbing ones full of the world's alarming symptoms, the old well-loved ones full of passages that I wish I had written, and the exciting new ones that make me doubt that I ever could.

I picked up Robert Frost's *Selected Poems*, its pages crammed with scraps of yellowed paper marking certain passages. Its cover is the color and texture of granite, edged with green. On the flyleaf the signature, "Robert Frost, Mount Holyoke, 1934," reminds me of the evening I nervously asked him to autograph my new copy. The handwriting looks shaky. He seemed an old man to me then, twenty-seven years ago, as he seems a young man to me now.

So I sat on the floor, marveling how the long years of youth telescope into the flicking years of middle age and how we can see a field whole only when we climb up a rocky pasture and look down at it from a distance.

Now that "I have to be gone for a season or so," I found myself measuring the shape of Vermont and wondering what it is that I miss and what I will search for when I return. As so often before, a line of Robert Frost's answered my question: "Good-bye and keep cold." He was talking about an apple orchard and the danger of a sudden thaw to young trees. But trees have been used as a symbol of life as long as man has sought for some meaning to his existence.

I've heard it said the Vermonters are cold. I suppose they are if you mean that they are not the least bit curious about your income, your religion, your prep school or college. In fourteen years I was never urged to join a church, a study group, or a gossip club. And this respect for the individual's right to think, act, and live as he sees fit is refreshingly cool.

I drove a red Ford truck for three years, not only to haul grain bags, bicycles, and skis but to carry me in my best bib and tucker to whatever social gathering I attended. No Vermonter ever seemed to see that truck except as a means of transportation.

I was never fawned on in a store because my husband had a position of responsibility nor was I ignored when my pedigree was not showing. In all those years no driver with Vermont license plates ever honked when I stalled after the light had turned green. I have been hubcap deep in sand, snow, and mud, and the first car along has always stopped

Good-bye and Keep Cold

and pulled me out. But these Samaritans never offered advice, criticism, or asked questions. They simply helped.

Our nearest neighbor never entertained us or was entertained by us, but she fed my children, sent over the first corn, or left a pie on the kitchen counter to welcome us home when we returned from a trip.

There is a lot of heat in the world that seems to generate only further friction and fear. I am already aware of the fallout from it in the metropolitan area. So, before I become contaminated or even enervated by the "warmth" of this new environment, I must look back at Vermont with the love and gratitude I could not speak as a Vermonter and say, "Good-bye and keep cold."

Epilogue

But now, eleven years after we said good-bye to Vermont, we're back to stay for all seasons. Vermont has kept cold, the cold it needs for the next season's growth, the silence of winter that hones the spirit. It is all very simple and goes way back to Antaeus, who was the child of the sea, as we all once were. He became stronger when he touched the earth. And so do we.

171